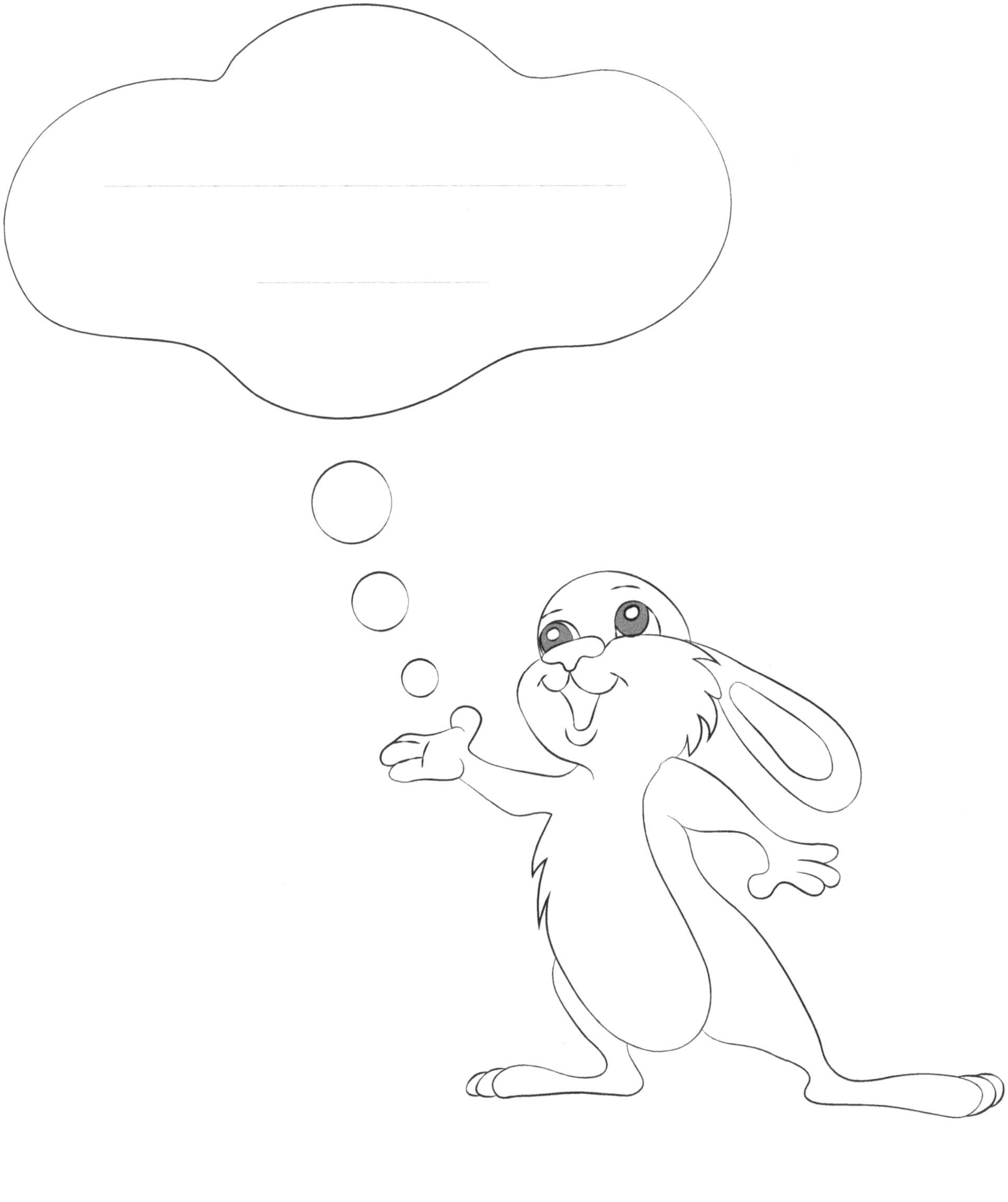

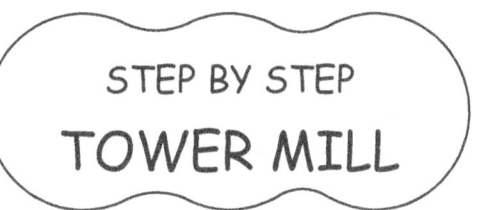

STEP BY STEP
TOWER MILL

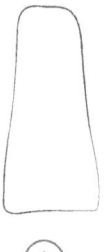

①

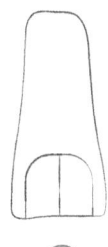

②

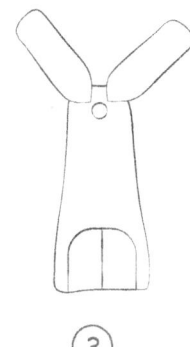

③

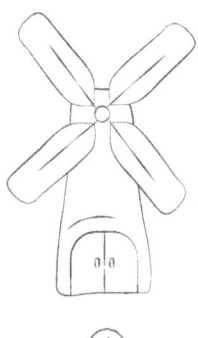

④

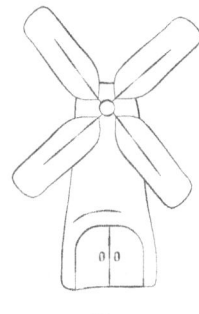

⑤

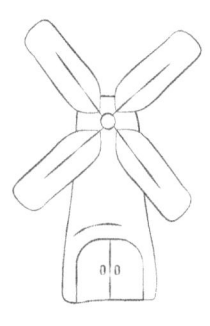

⑥

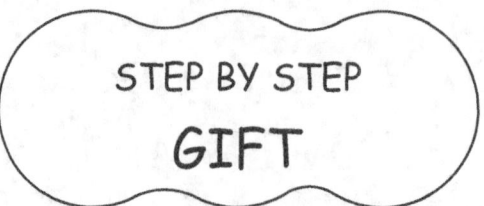

STEP BY STEP
GIFT

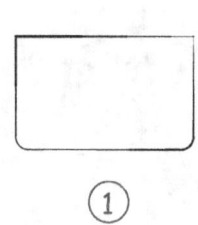

①

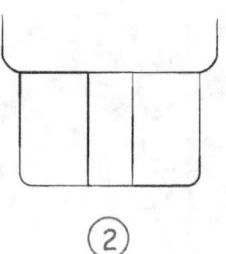

②

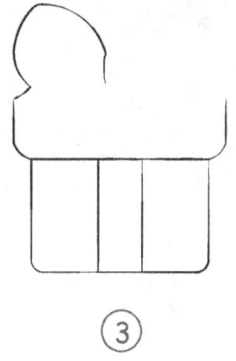

③

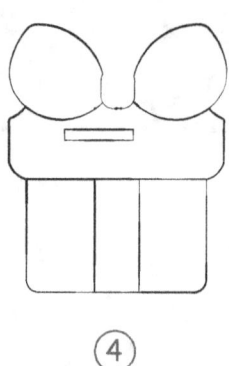

④

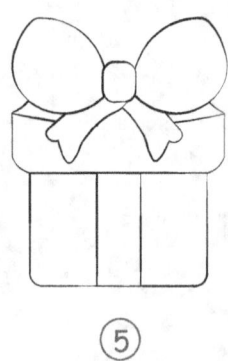

⑤

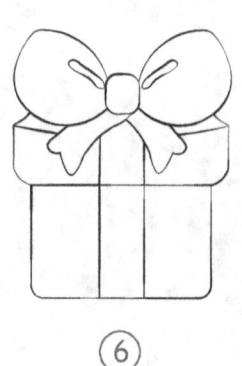

⑥

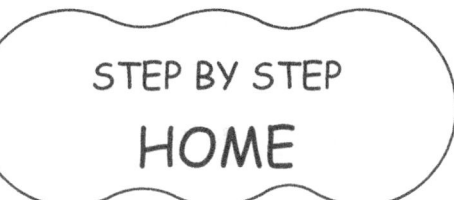

STEP BY STEP
HOME

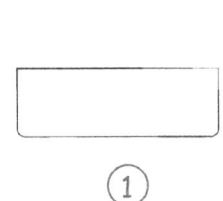

①

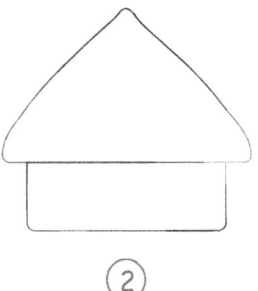

②

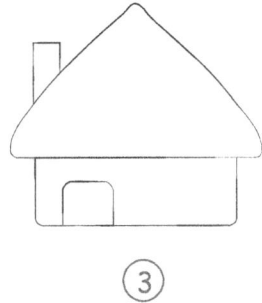

③

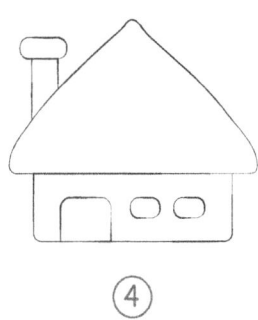

④

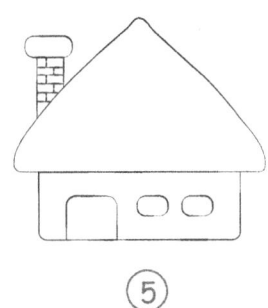

⑤

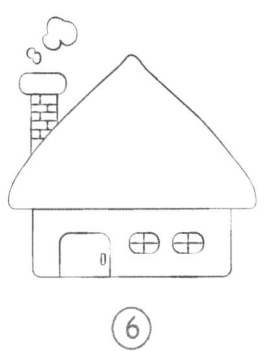

⑥

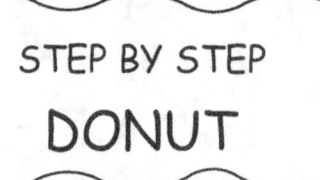

STEP BY STEP
DONUT

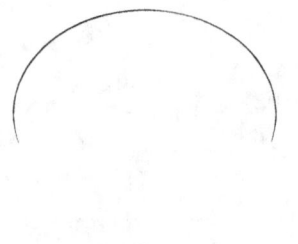

①

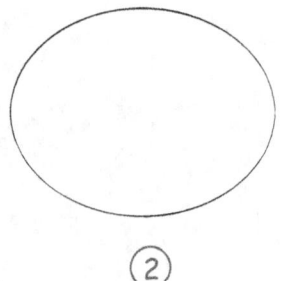

②

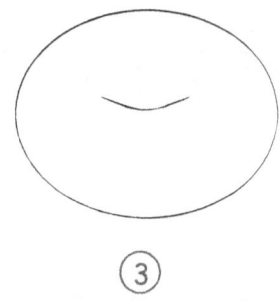

③

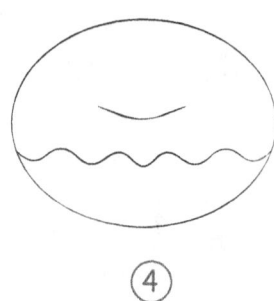

④

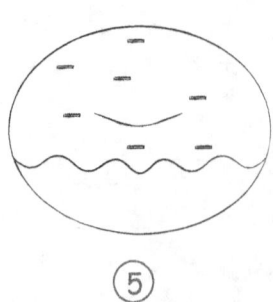

⑤

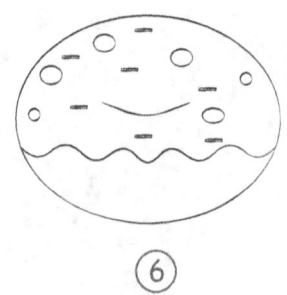

⑥

STEP BY STEP
CACTUS

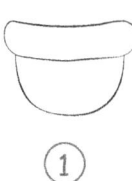

①

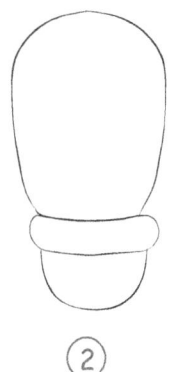

②

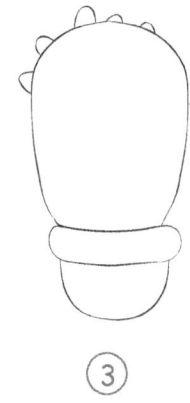

③

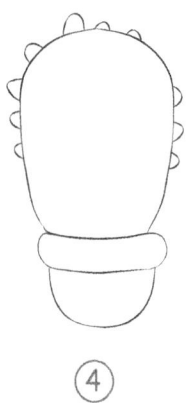

④

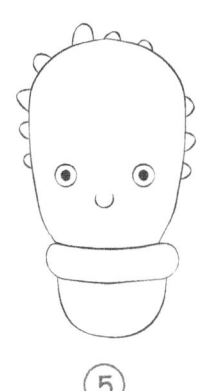

⑤

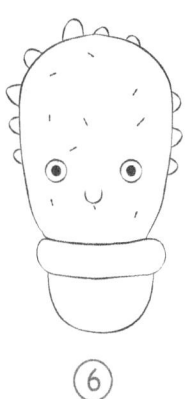

⑥

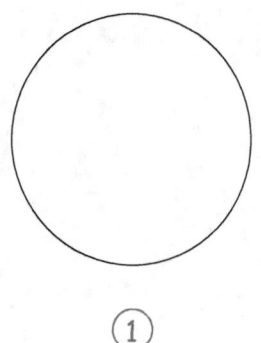

①

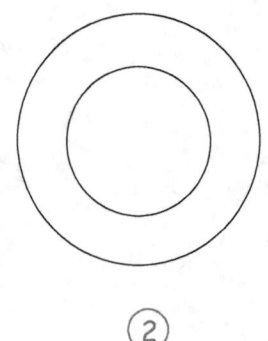

②

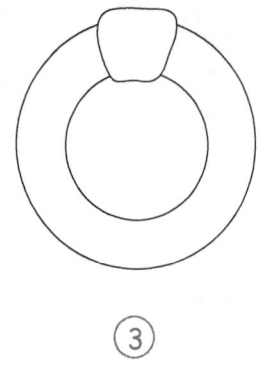

③

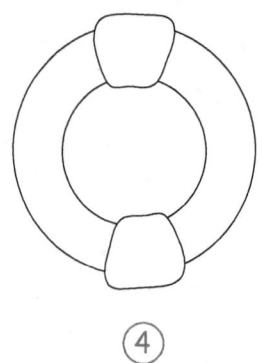

④

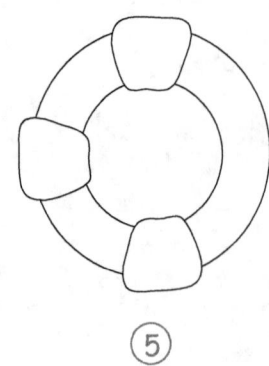

⑤

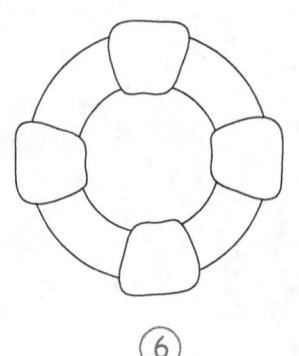

⑥

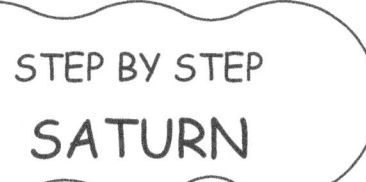

STEP BY STEP
SATURN

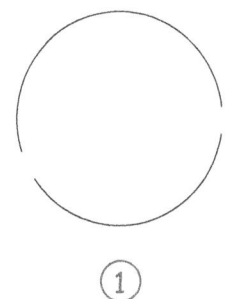

①

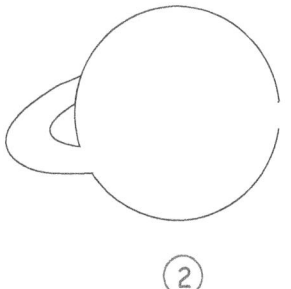

②

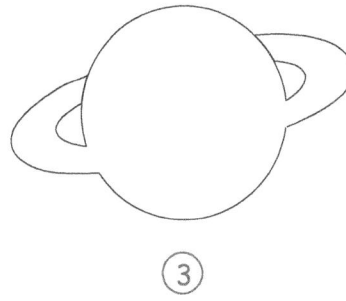

③

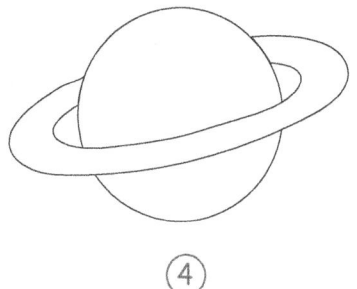

④

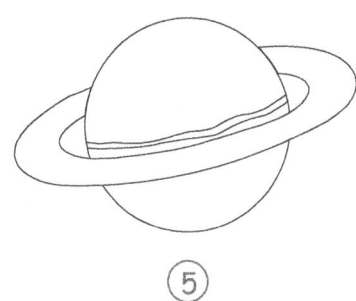

⑤

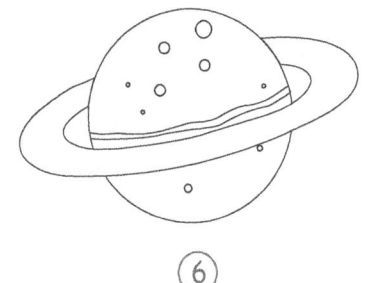

⑥

STEP BY STEP
GOGGLES

① ②

③ ④

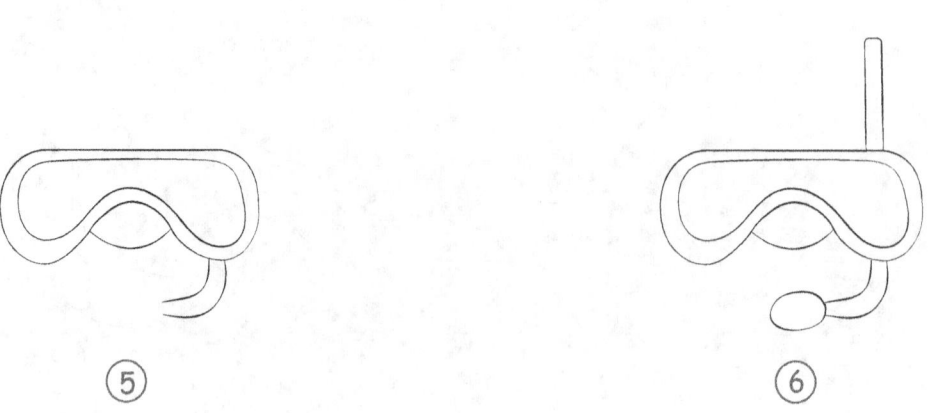

⑤ ⑥

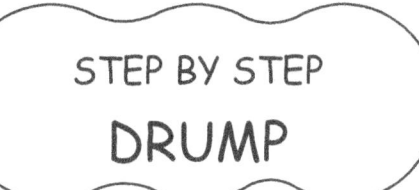

STEP BY STEP
DRUMP

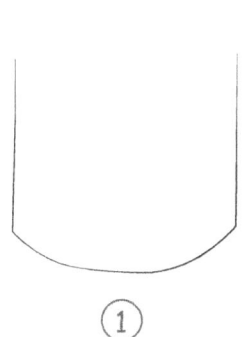

①

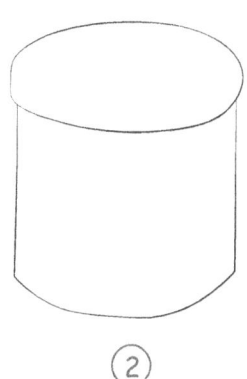

②

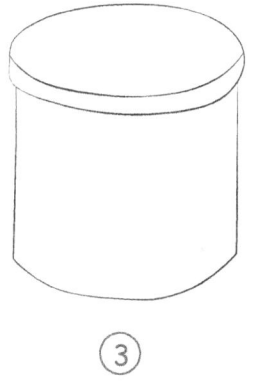

③

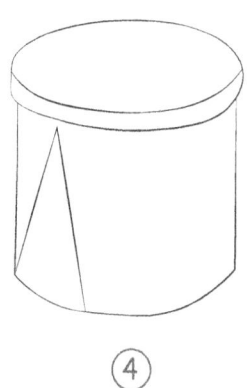

④

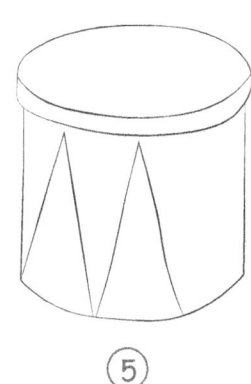

⑤

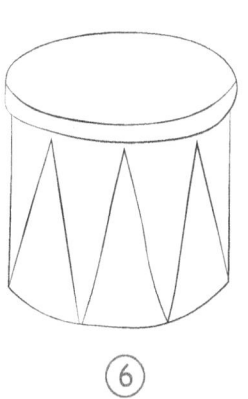

⑥

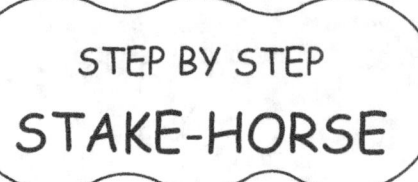

STEP BY STEP
STAKE-HORSE

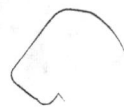

①

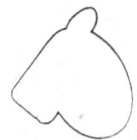

②

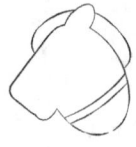

③

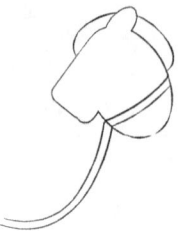

④

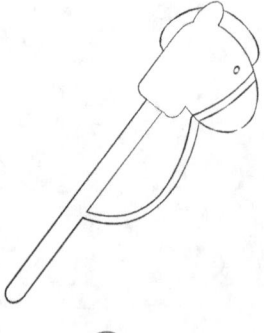

⑤

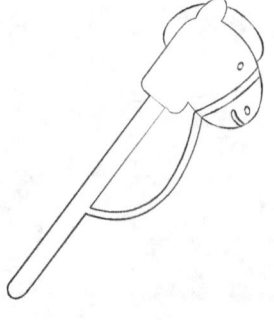

⑥

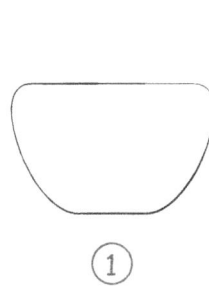

①

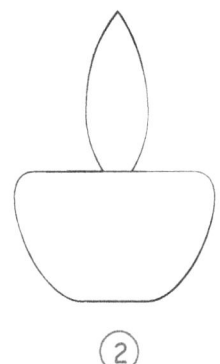

②

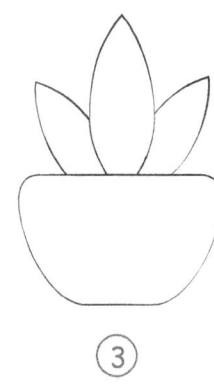

③

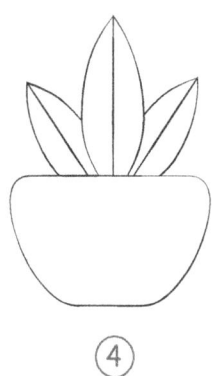

④

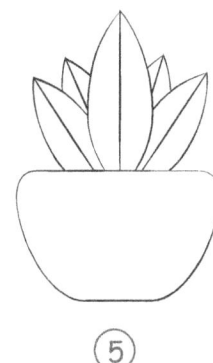

⑤

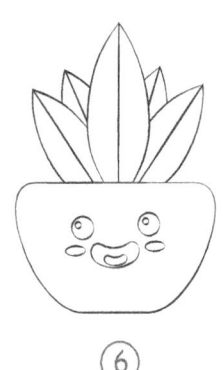

⑥

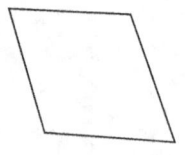

①

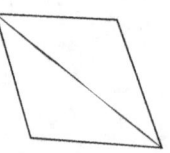

②

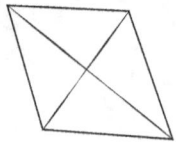

③

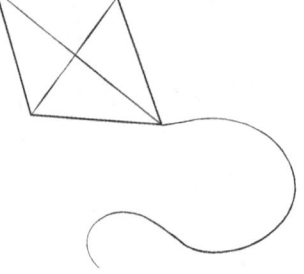

④

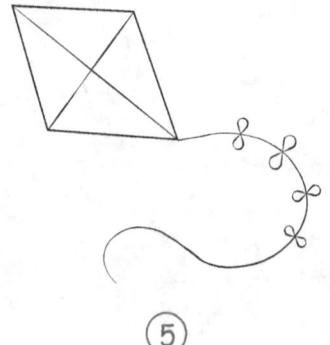

⑤

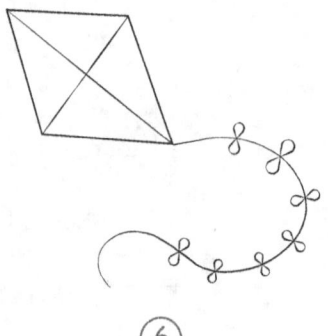

⑥

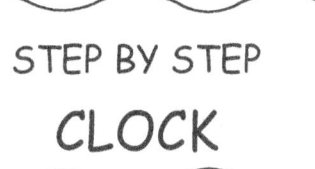

STEP BY STEP
CLOCK

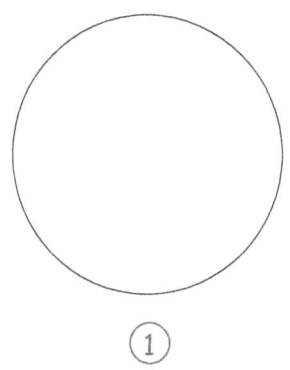

①

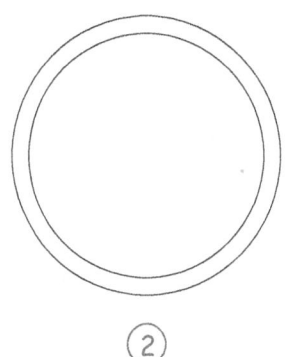

②

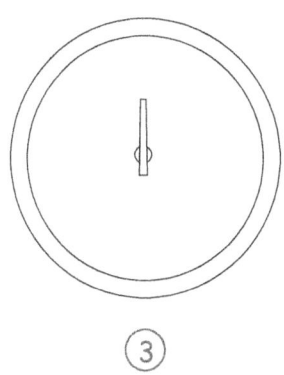

③

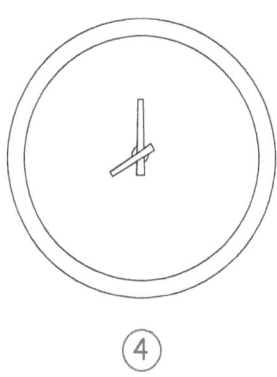

④

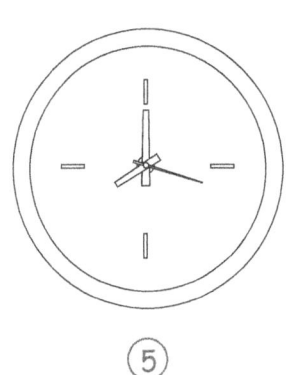

⑤

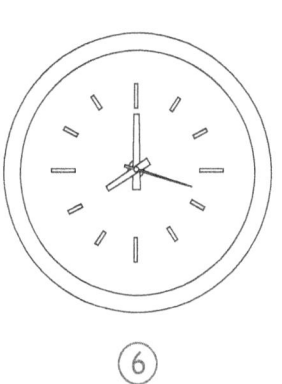

⑥

STEP BY STEP
PENCIL

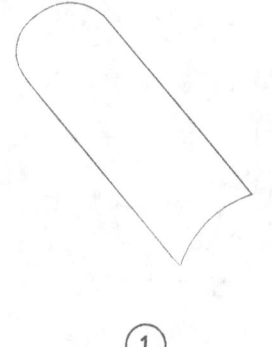

①

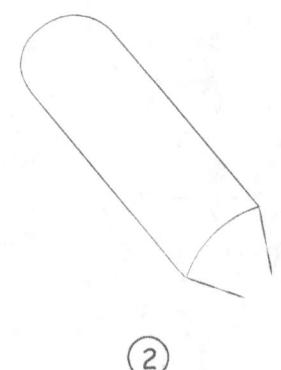

②

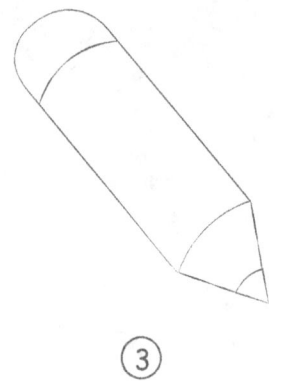

③

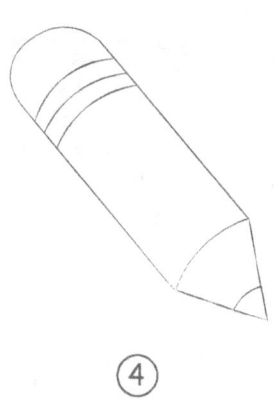

④

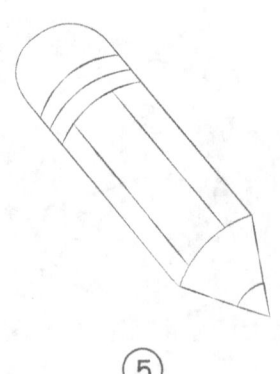

⑤

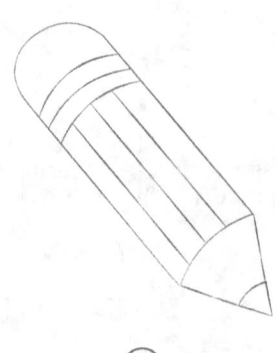

⑥

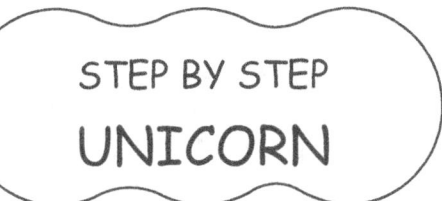

STEP BY STEP
UNICORN

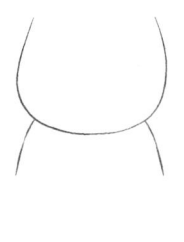

①

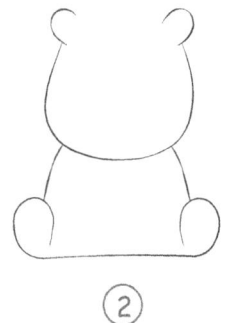

②

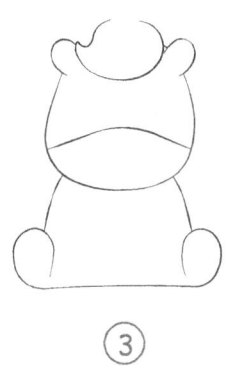

③

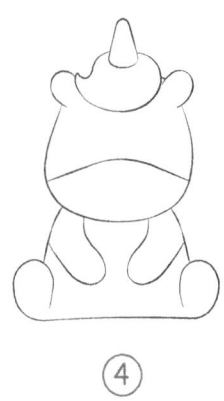

④

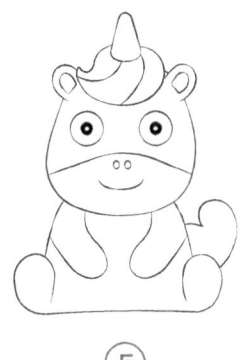

⑤

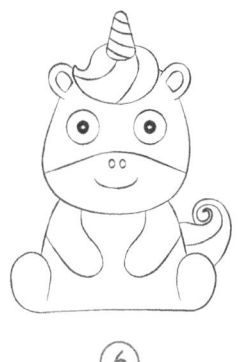

⑥

①

②

③

④

⑤

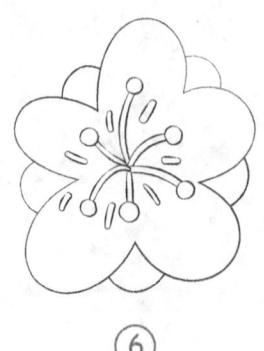

⑥

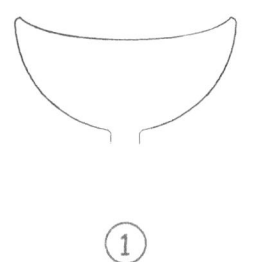

①

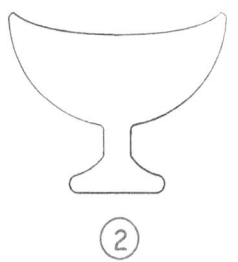

②

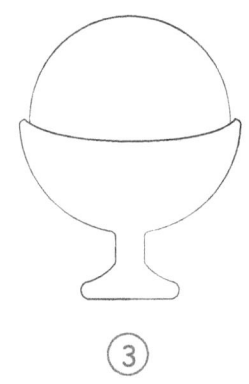

③

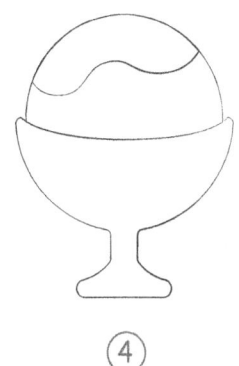

④

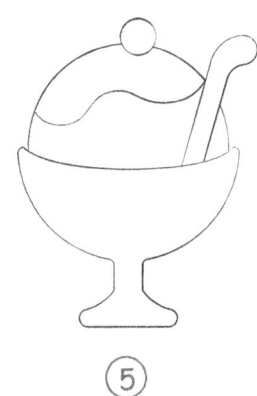

⑤

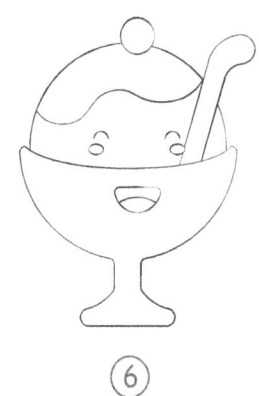

⑥

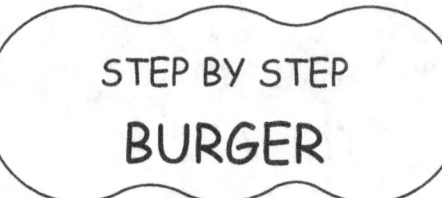

STEP BY STEP
BURGER

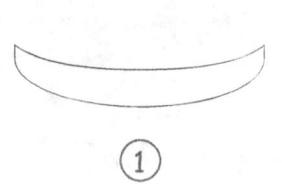

①

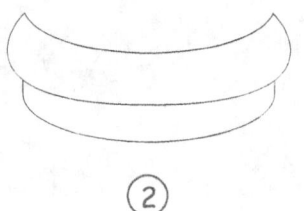

②

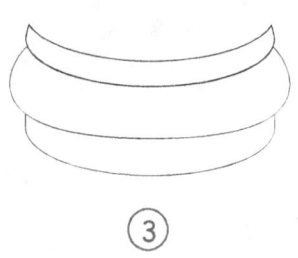

③

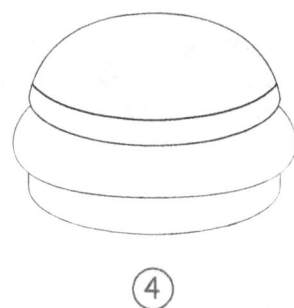

④

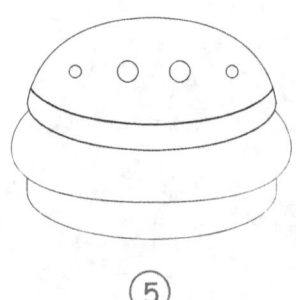

⑤

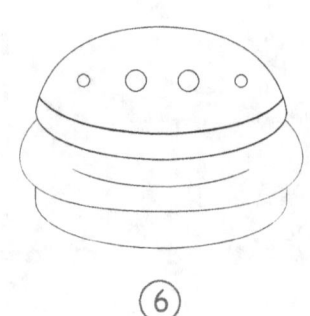

⑥

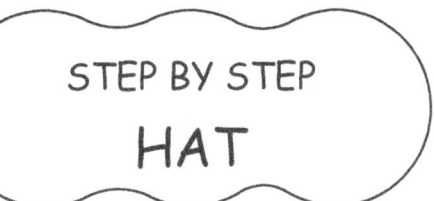

STEP BY STEP
HAT

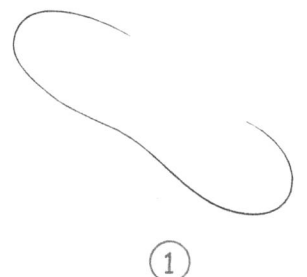

①

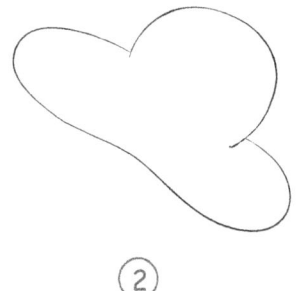

②

③

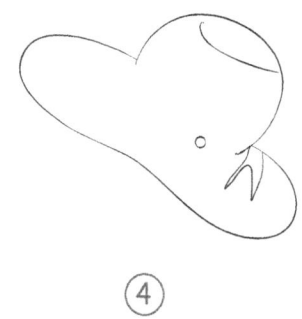

④

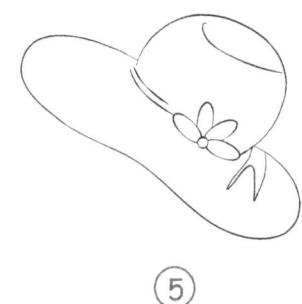

⑤

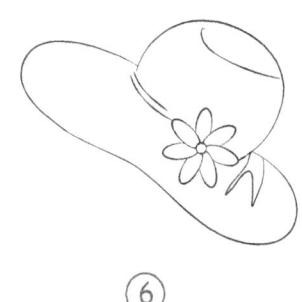

⑥

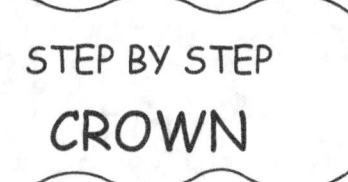

①

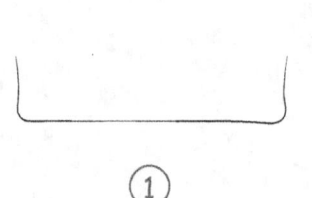

②

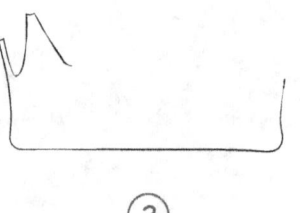

③

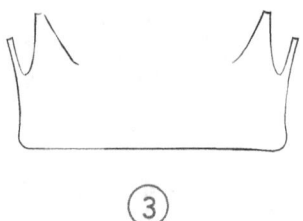

④

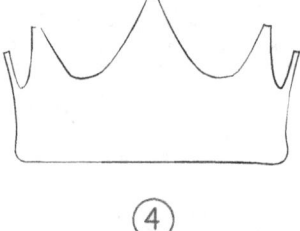

⑤

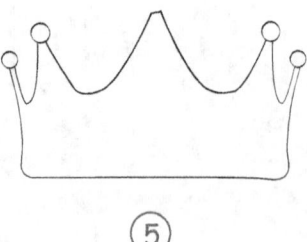

⑥

STEP BY STEP

HOT AIR BALLOON

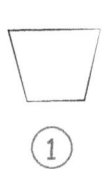

①

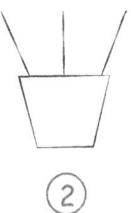

②

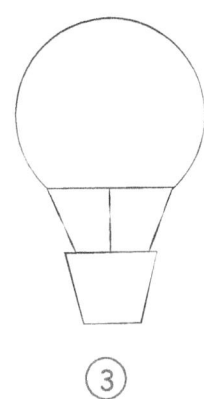

③

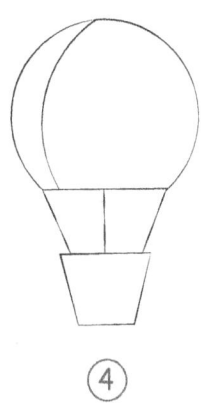

④

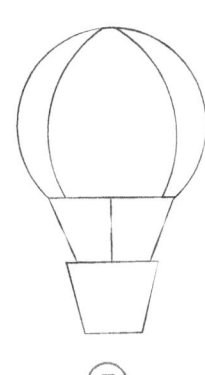

⑤

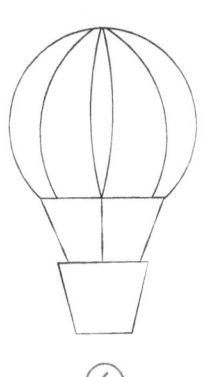

⑥

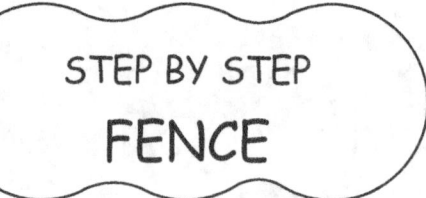

STEP BY STEP
FENCE

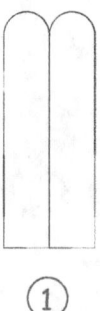

①

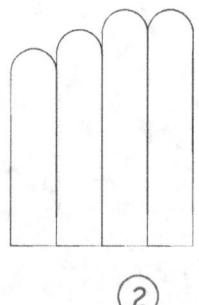

②

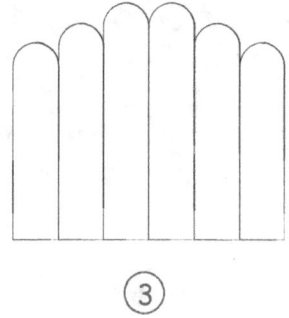

③

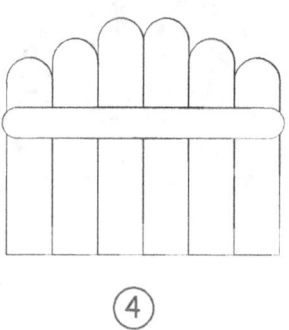

④

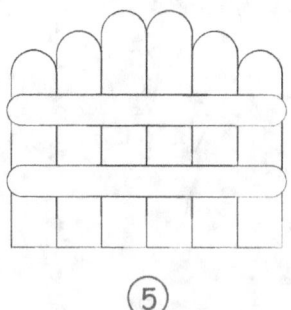

⑤

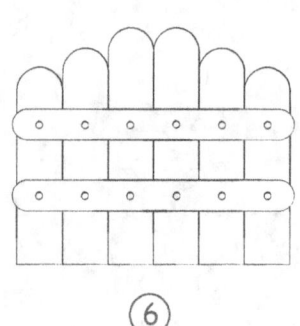

⑥

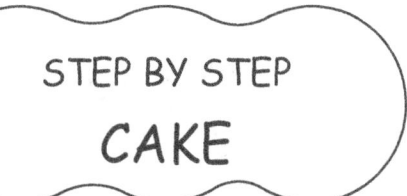

STEP BY STEP
CAKE

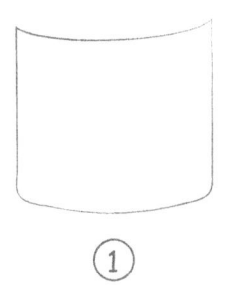

①

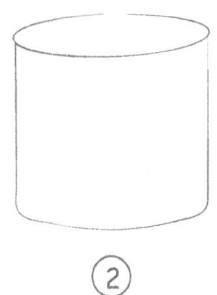

②

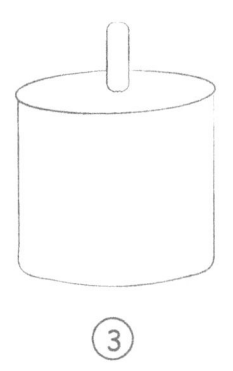

③

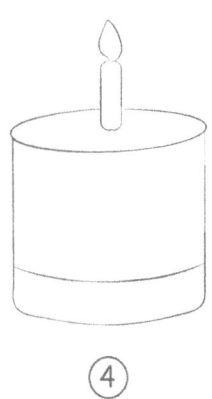

④

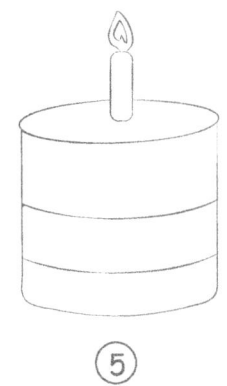

⑤

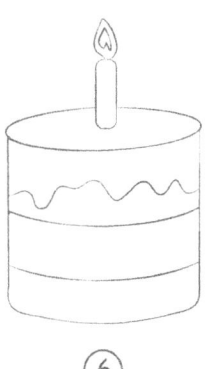

⑥

STEP BY STEP
GUITAR

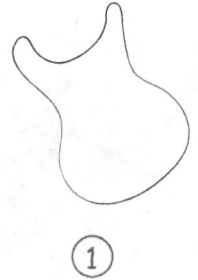

(1)

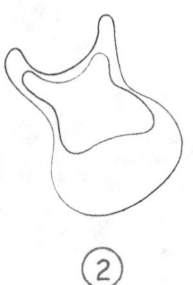

(2)

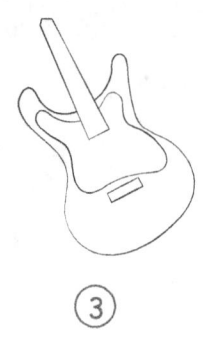

(3)

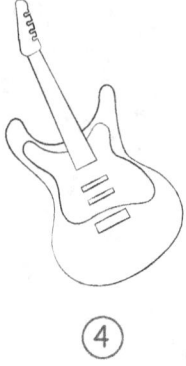

(4)

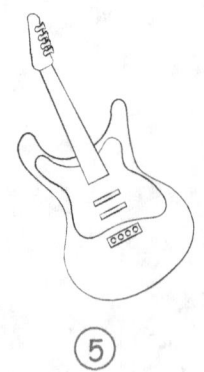

(5)

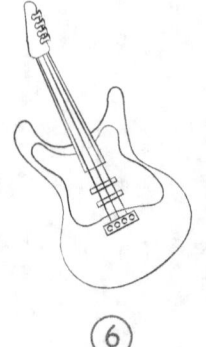

(6)

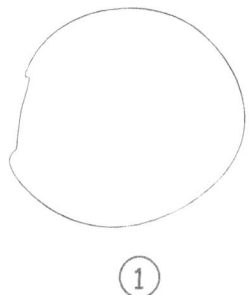

①

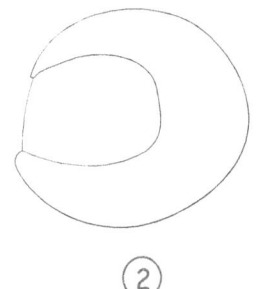

②

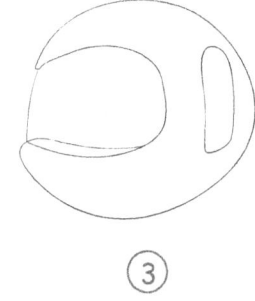

③

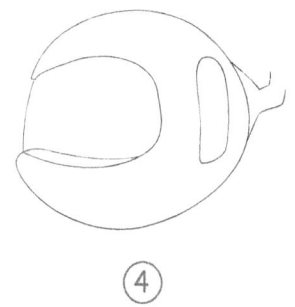

④

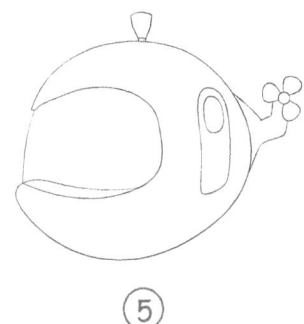

⑤

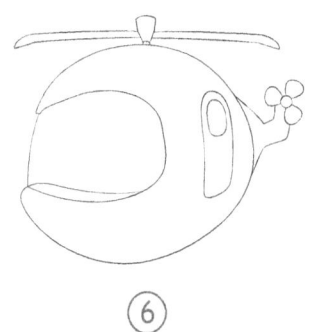

⑥

①

②

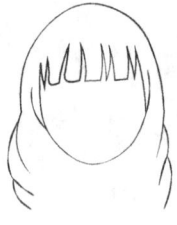

③

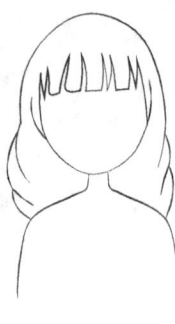

④

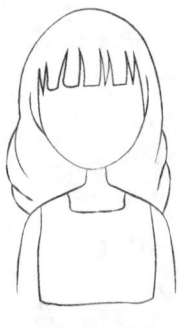

⑤

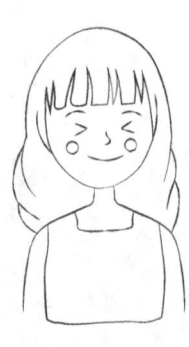

⑥

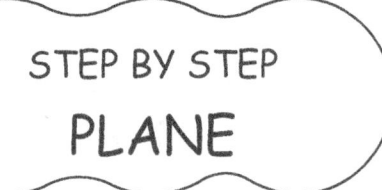

STEP BY STEP
PLANE

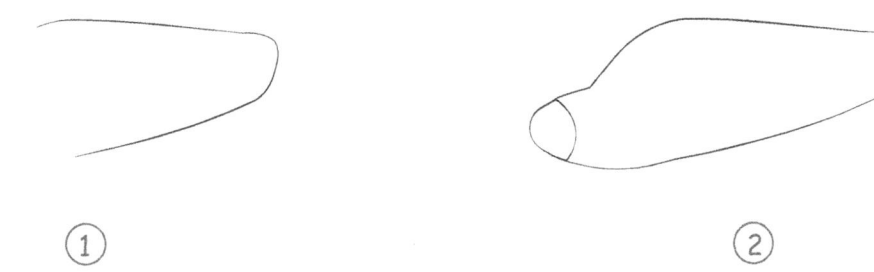

①

②

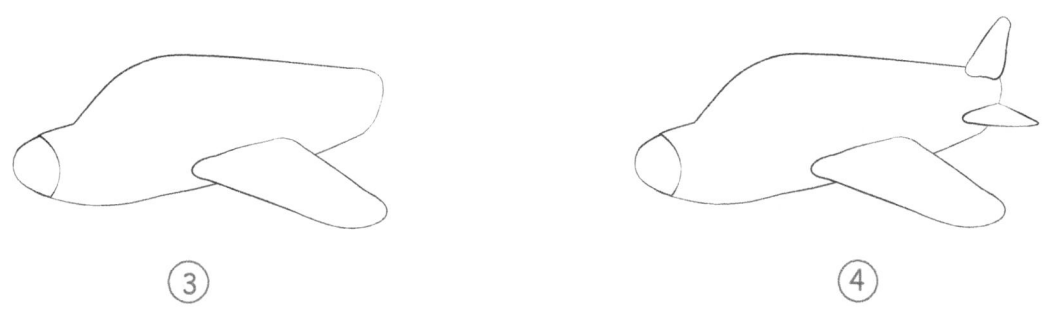

③

④

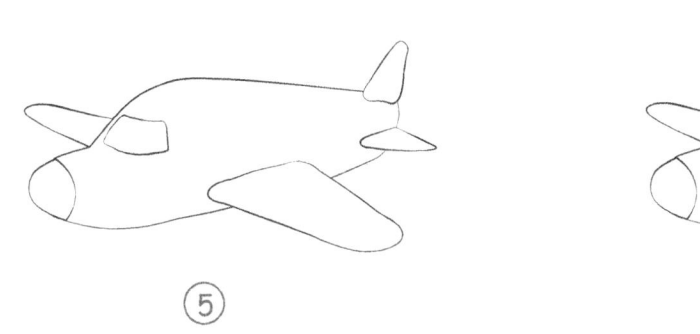

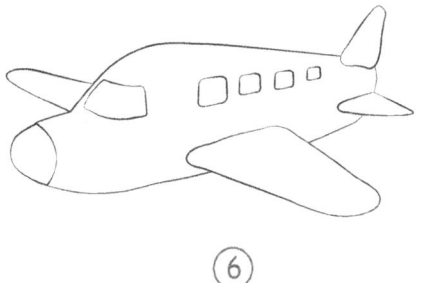

⑤

⑥

STEP BY STEP
MICROPHONE

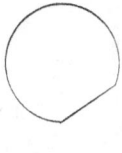

①

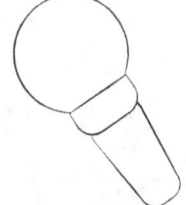

②

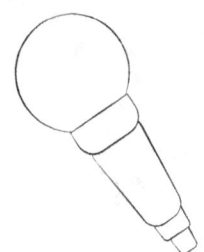

③

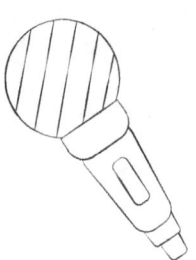

④

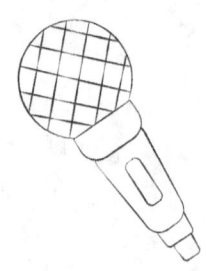

⑤

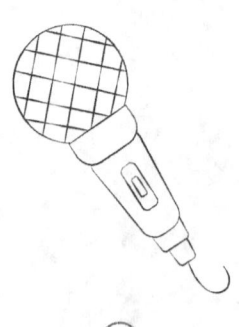

⑥

STEP BY STEP
SPIDER

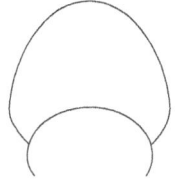

①

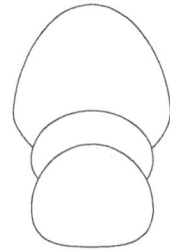

②

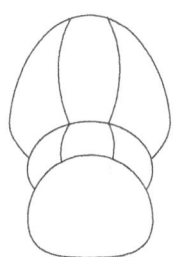

③

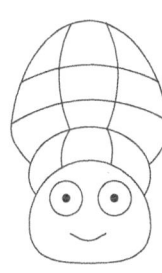

④

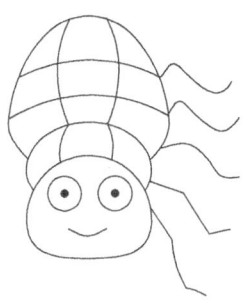

⑤

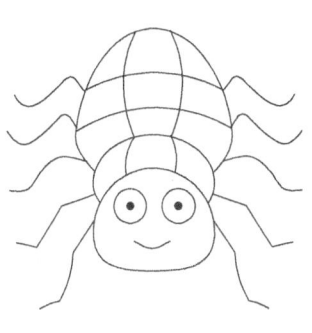

⑥

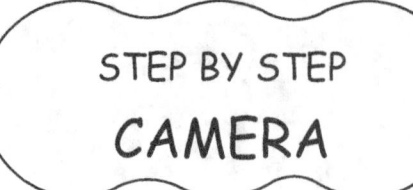

STEP BY STEP
CAMERA

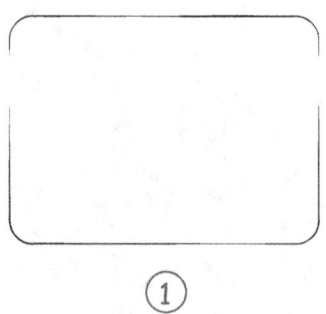

①

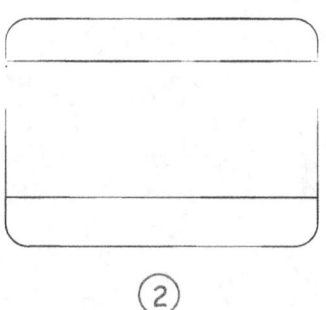

②

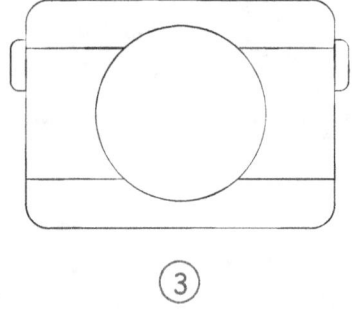

③

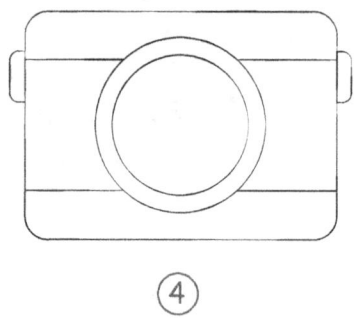

④

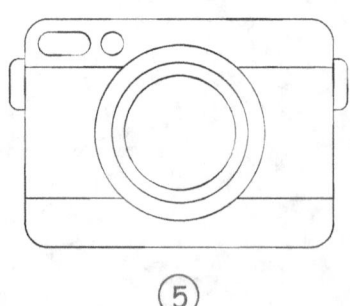

⑤

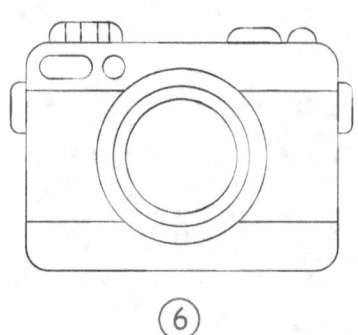

⑥

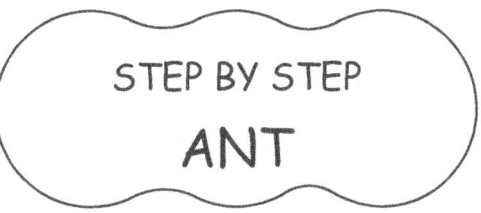

STEP BY STEP
ANT

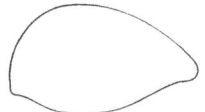

①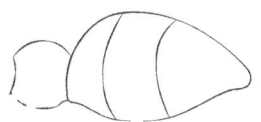

②

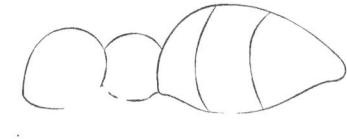

③

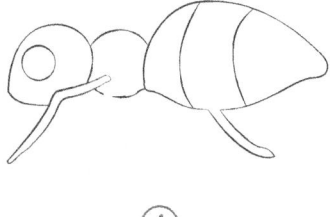

④

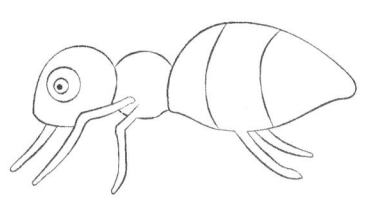

⑤

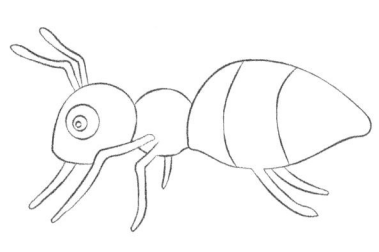

⑥

STEP BY STEP
FRIES

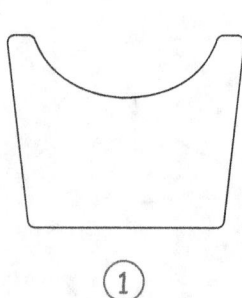

①

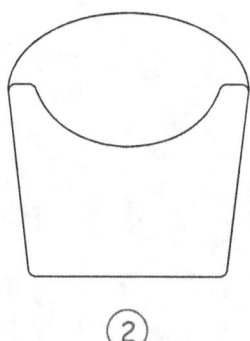

②

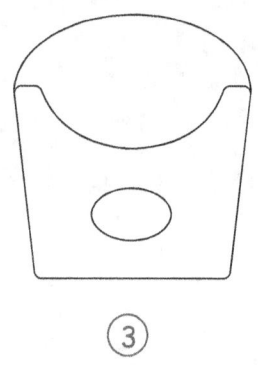

③

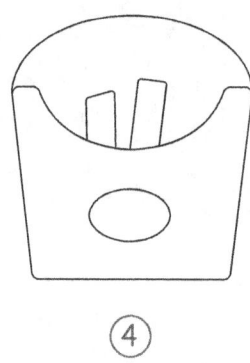

④

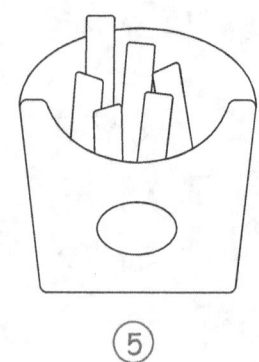

⑤

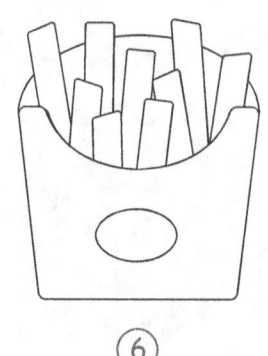

⑥

STEP BY STEP
SNAIL

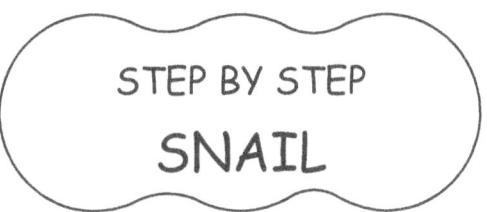

① ②

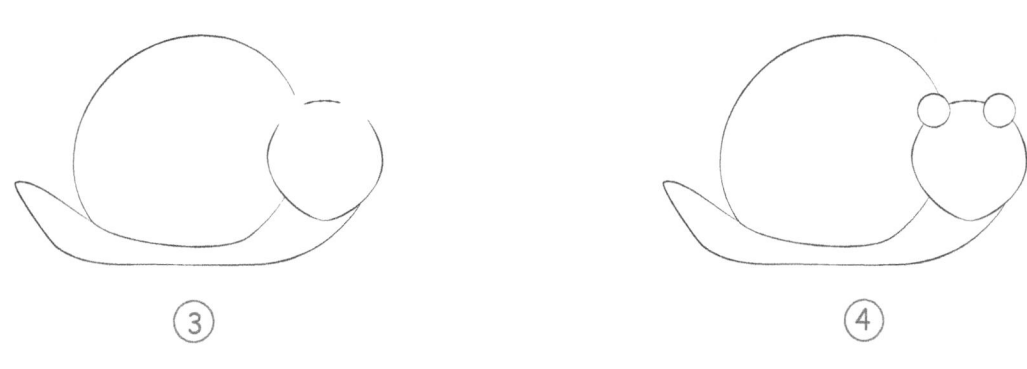

③ ④

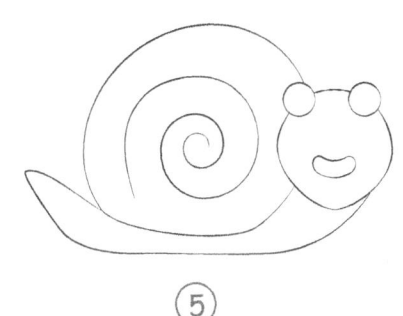 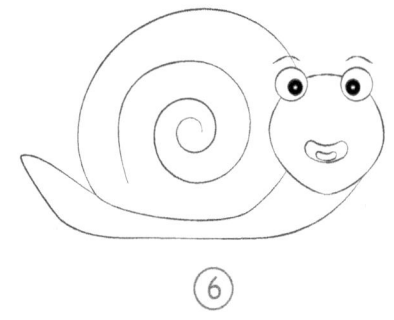

⑤ ⑥

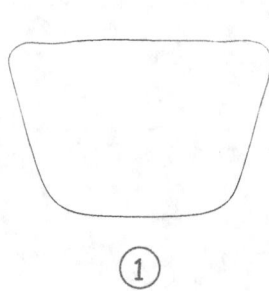

①

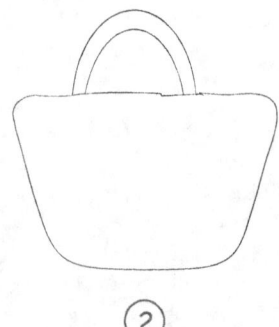

②

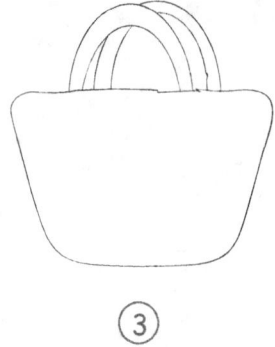

③

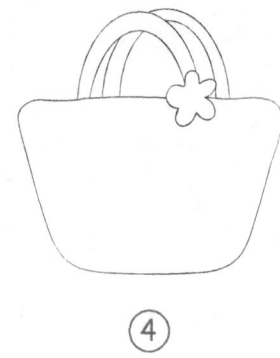

④

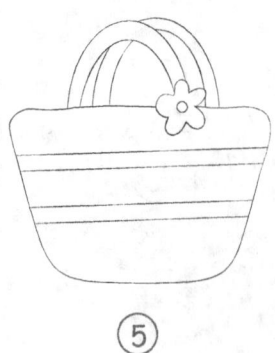

⑤

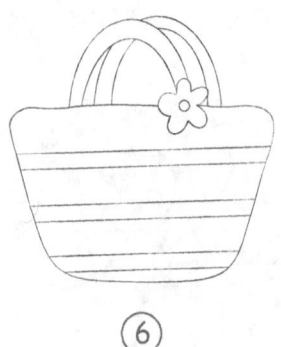

⑥

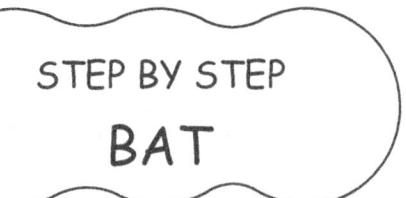

STEP BY STEP
BAT

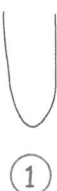

①

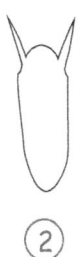

②

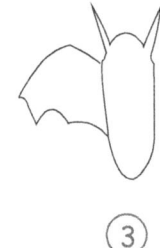

③

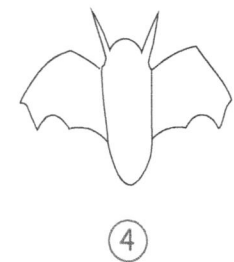

④

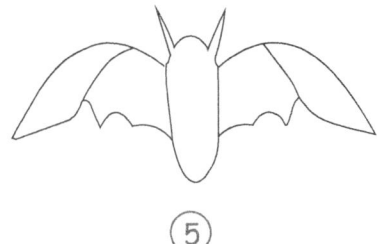

⑤

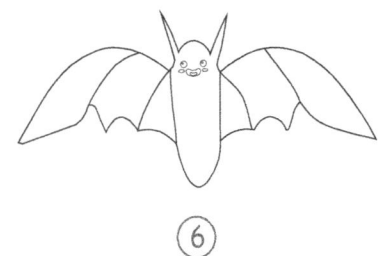

⑥

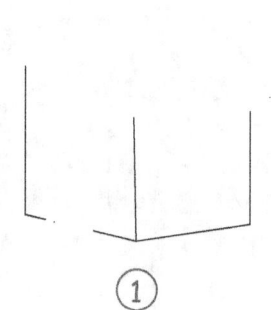

①

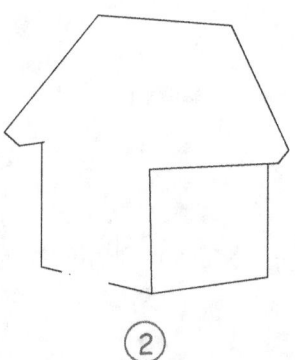

②

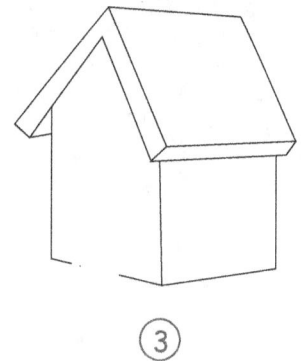

③

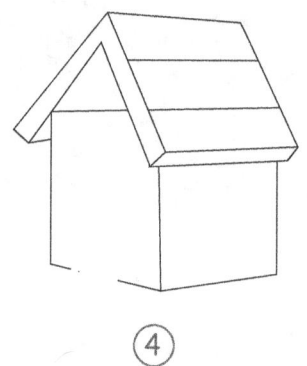

④

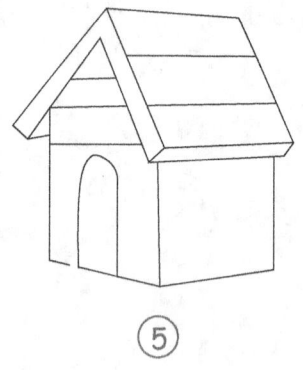

⑤

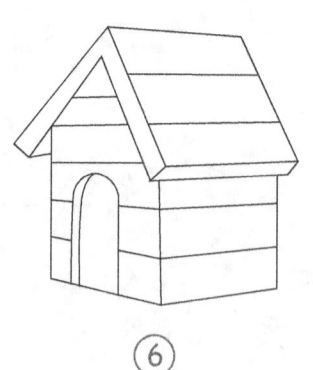

⑥

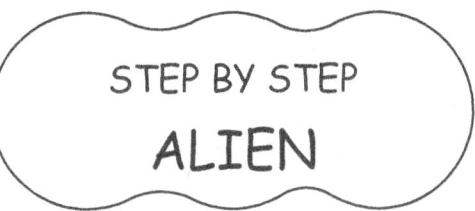

STEP BY STEP
ALIEN

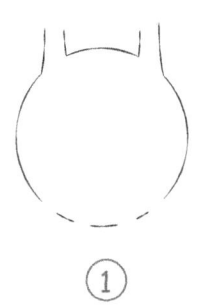

①

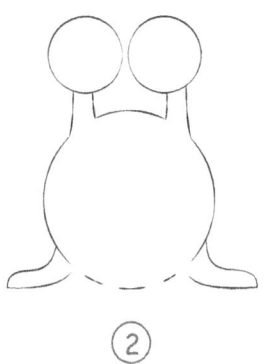

②

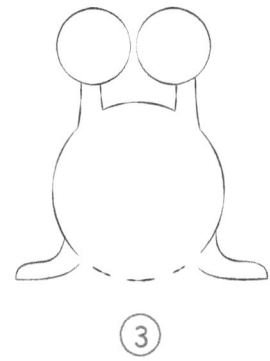

③

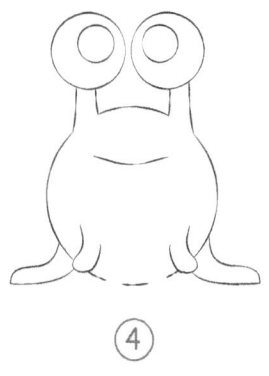

④

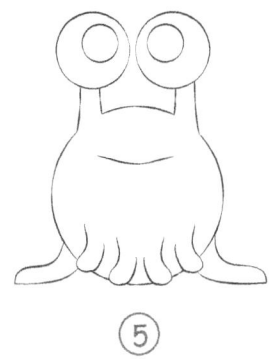

⑤

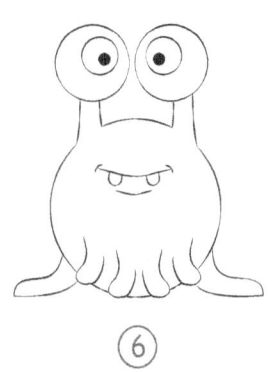

⑥

STEP BY STEP
MONSTER

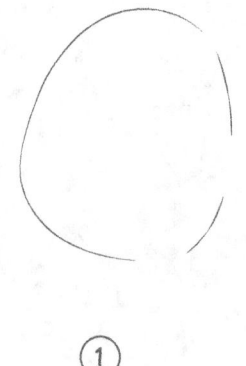

①

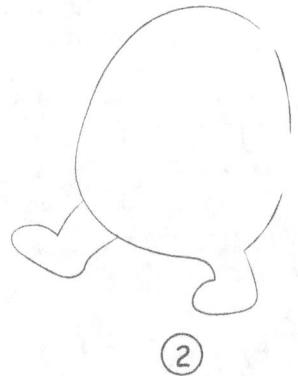

②

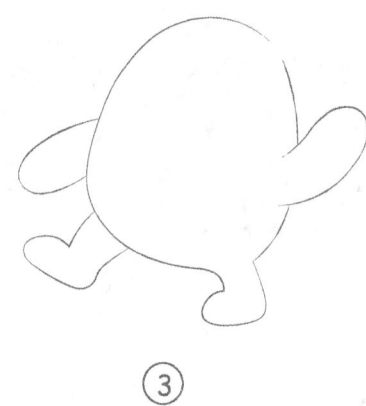

③

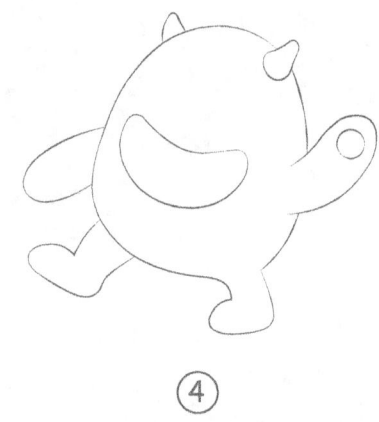

④

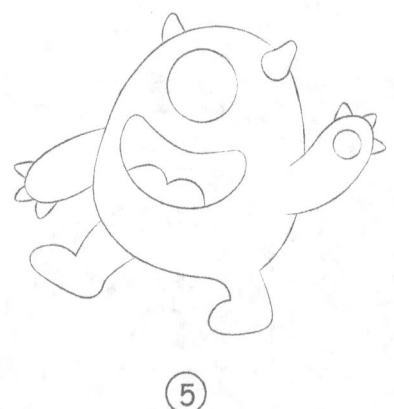

⑤

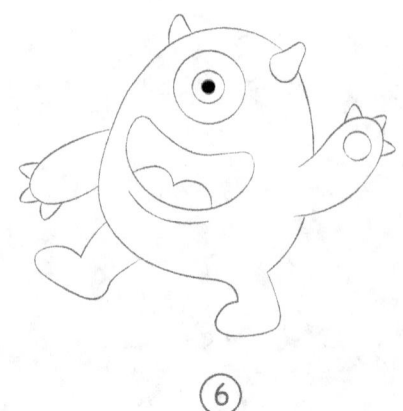

⑥

STEP BY STEP
UMBRELLA

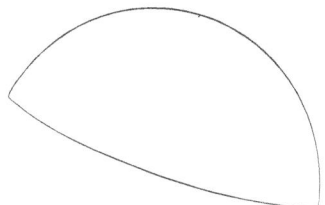

①

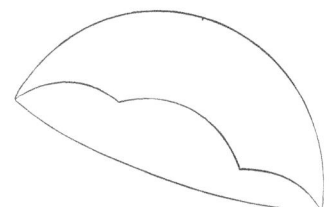

②

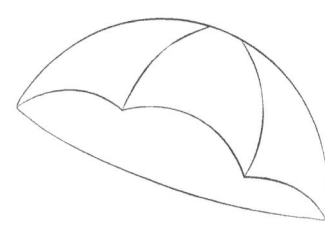

③

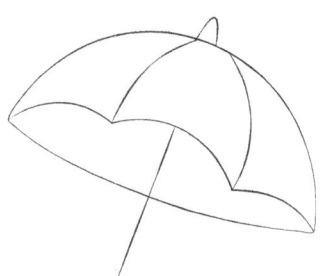

④

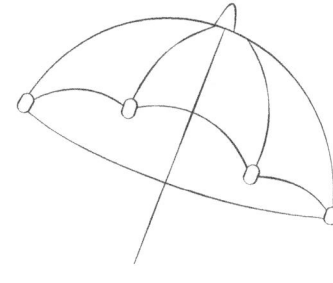

⑤

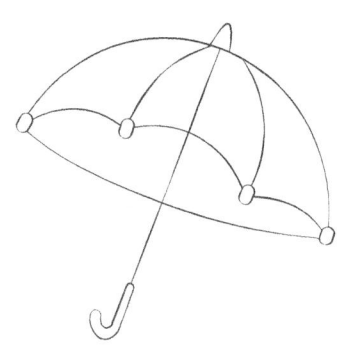

⑥

STEP BY STEP
MONSTER

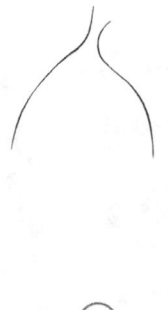

①

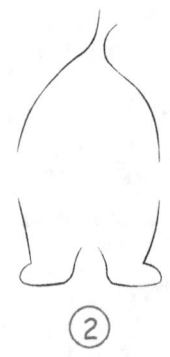

②

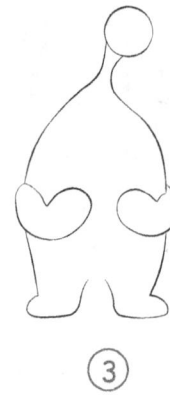

③

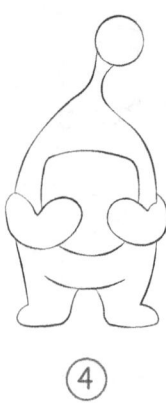

④

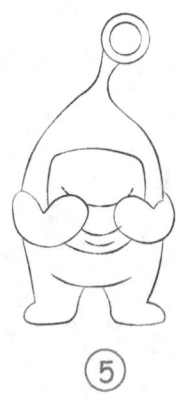

⑤

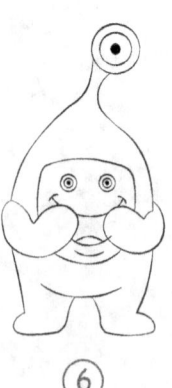

⑥

STEP BY STEP
GHOST

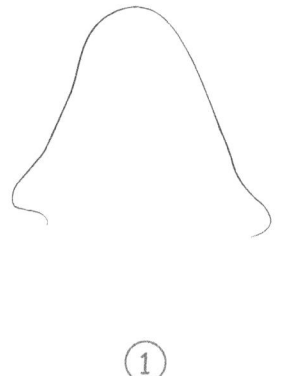

①

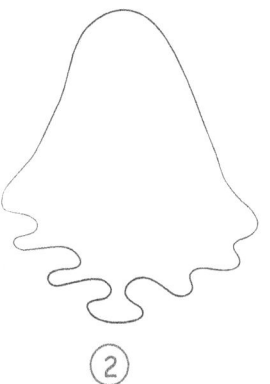

②

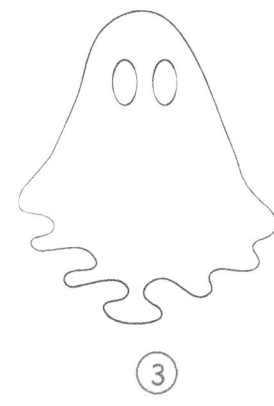

③

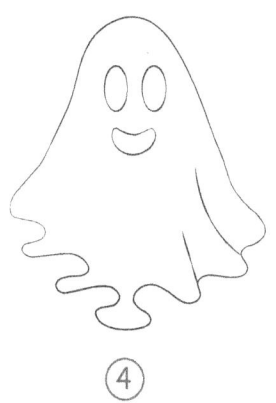

④

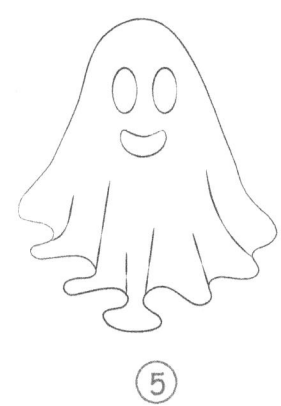

⑤

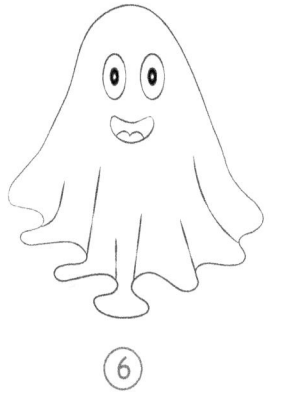

⑥

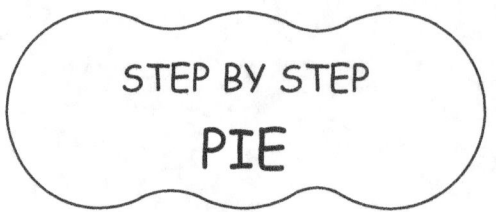

STEP BY STEP
PIE

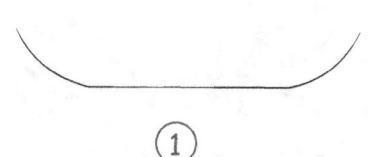

①

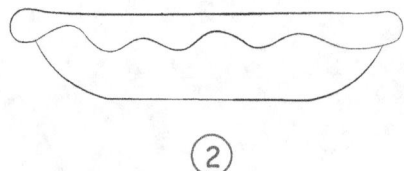

②

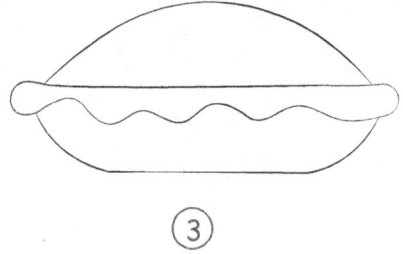

③

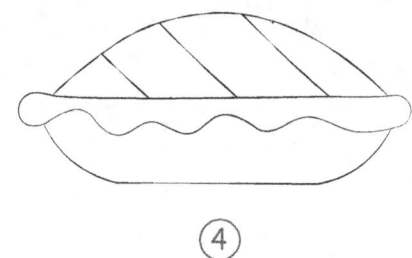

④

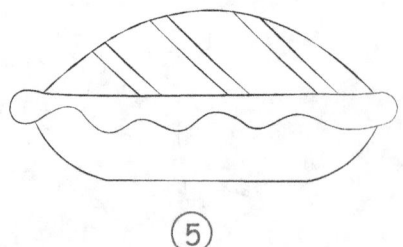

⑤

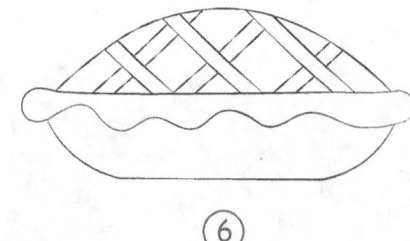

⑥

STEP BY STEP
CORN

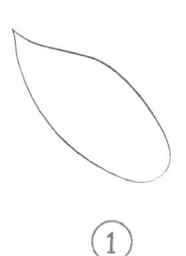

①

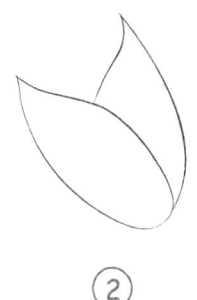

②

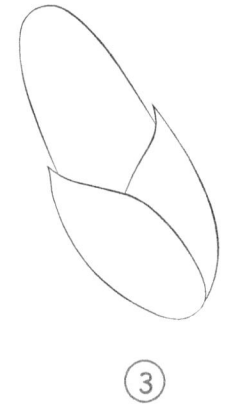

③

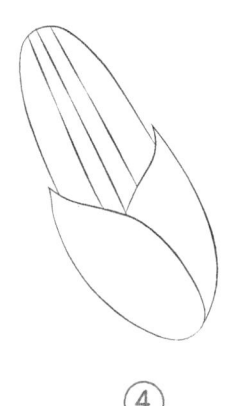

④

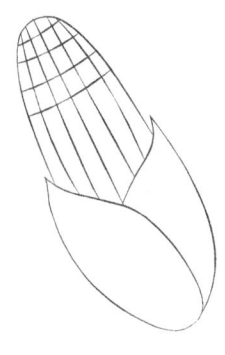

⑤

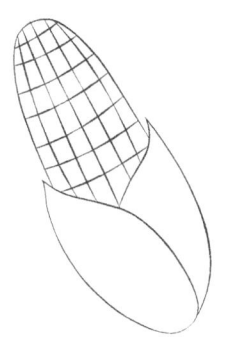

⑥

STEP BY STEP
PUMPKIN

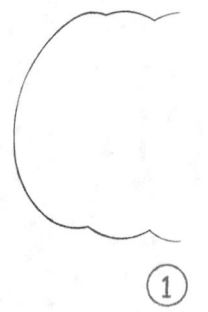

①

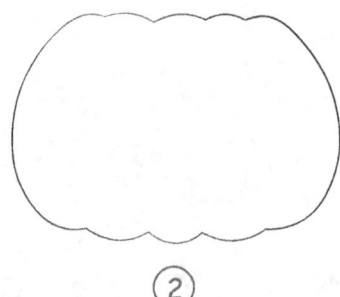

②

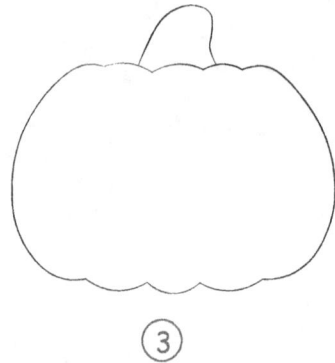

③

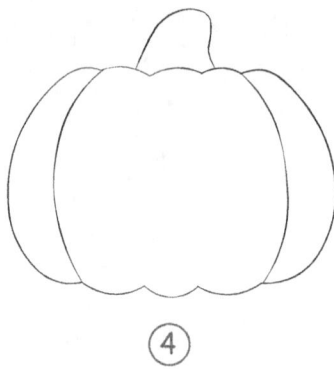

④

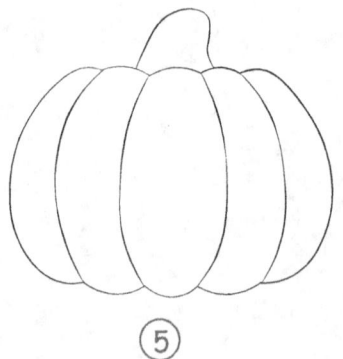

⑤

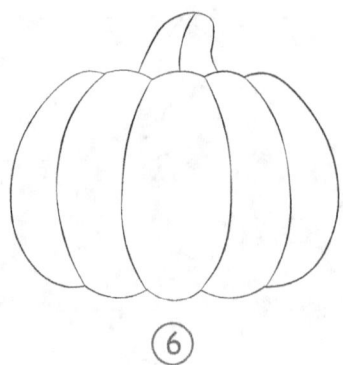

⑥

STEP BY STEP
FOOTBALL

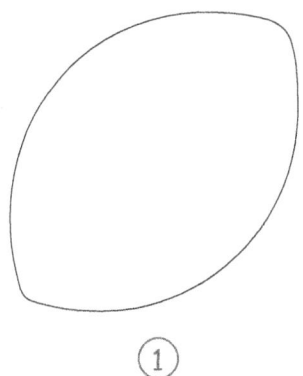

①

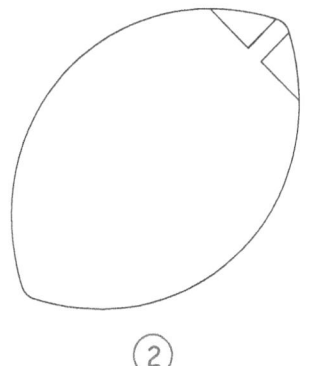

②

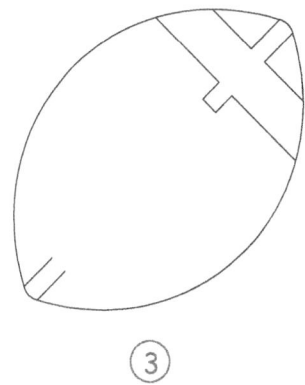

③

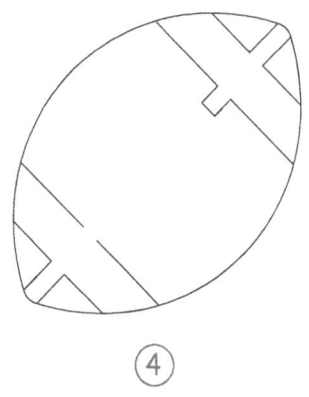

④

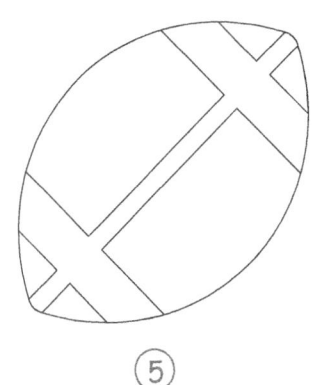

⑤

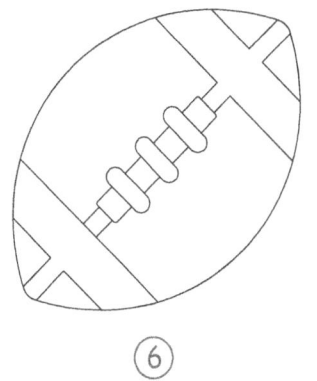

⑥

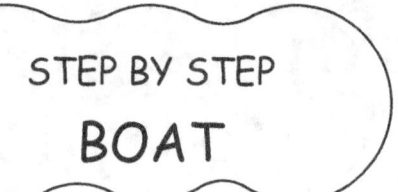

STEP BY STEP
BOAT

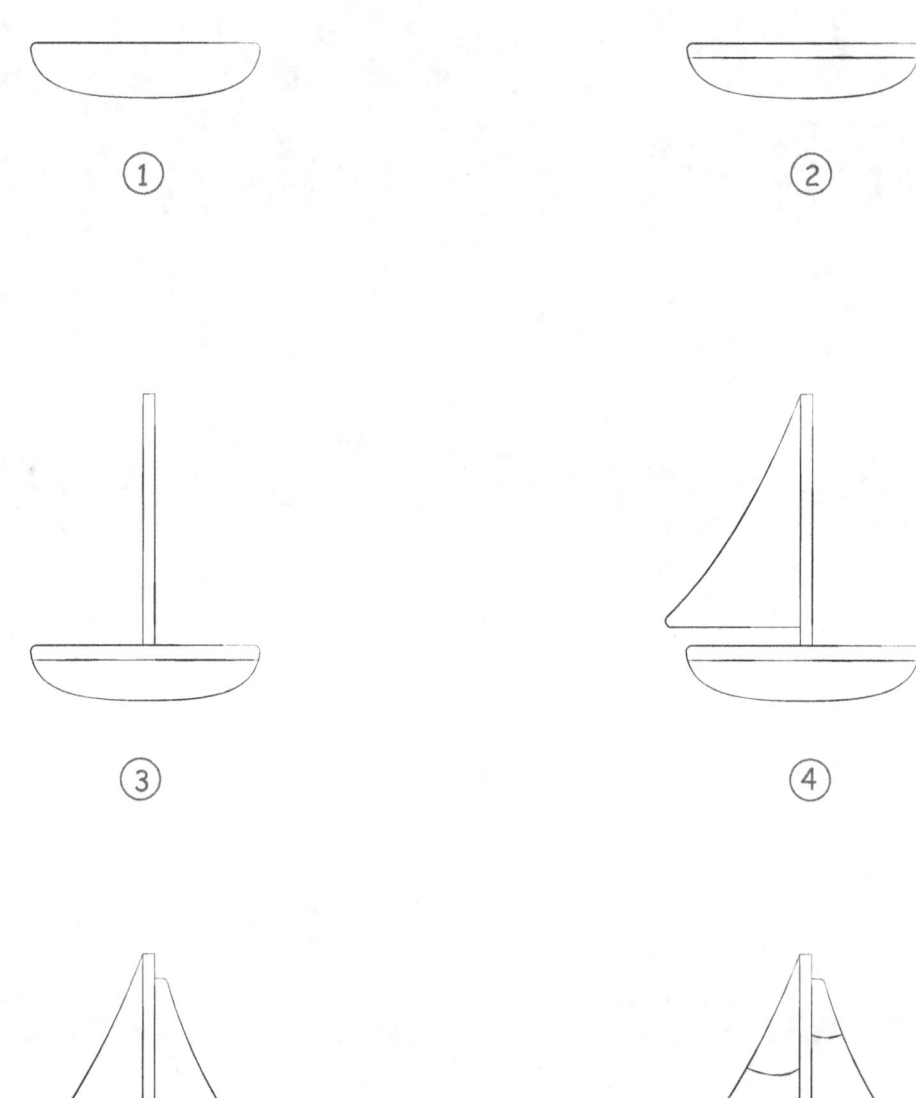

① ② ③ ④ ⑤ ⑥

STEP BY STEP
CUTE CUP

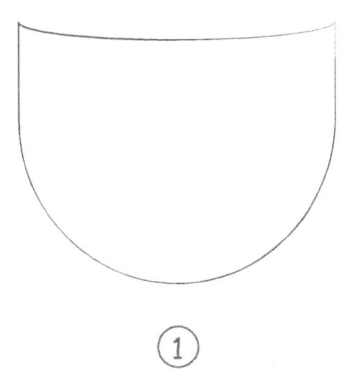

①

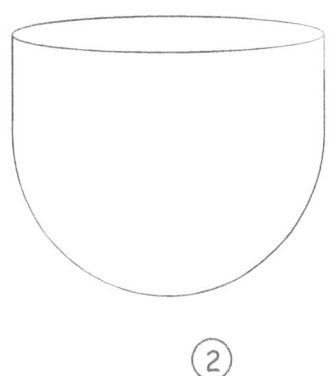

②

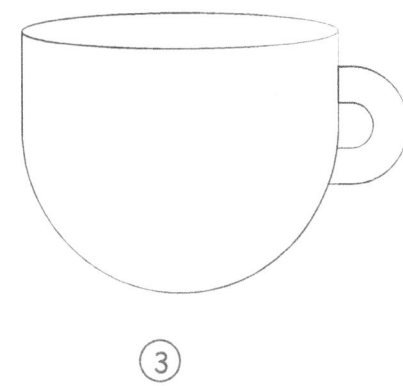

③

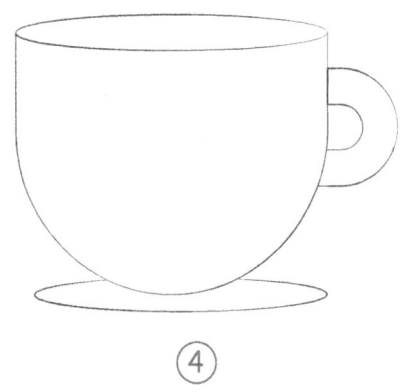

④

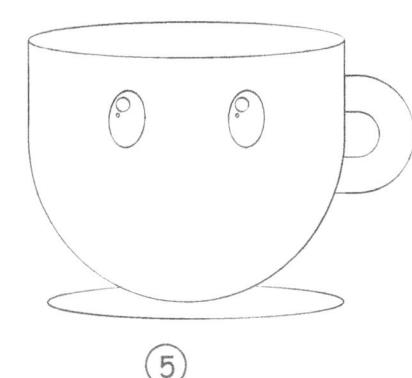

⑤

⑥

STEP BY STEP
WATERMELON

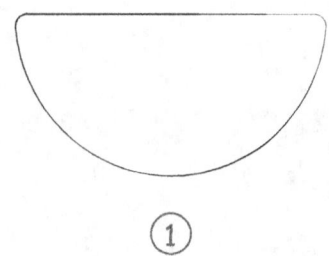

①

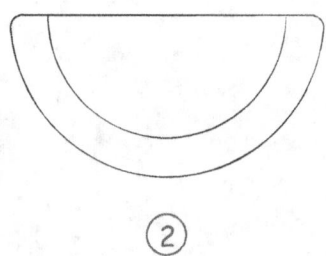

②

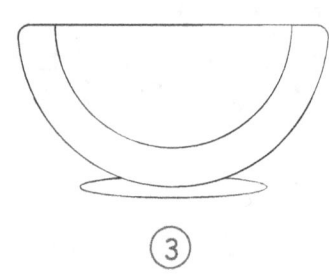

③

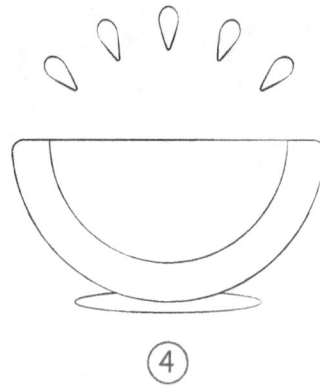

④

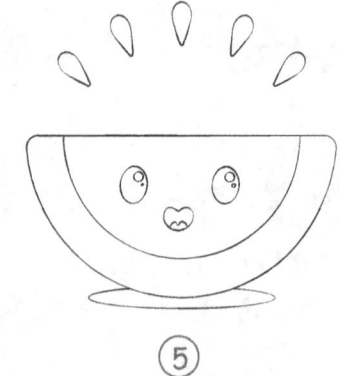

⑤

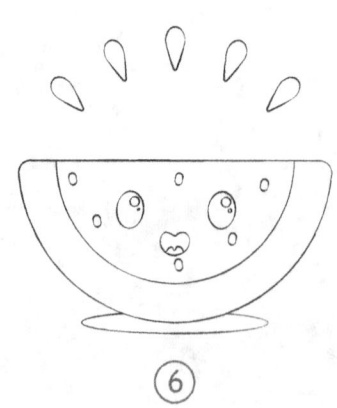

⑥

STEP BY STEP
MUSHROOM

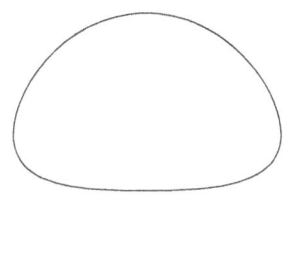

①

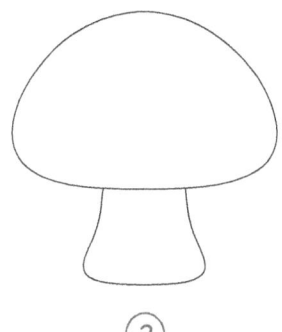

②

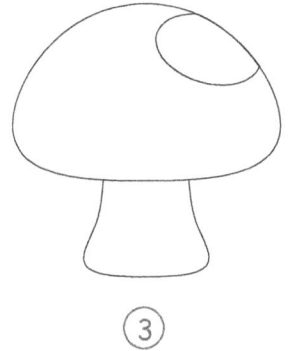

③

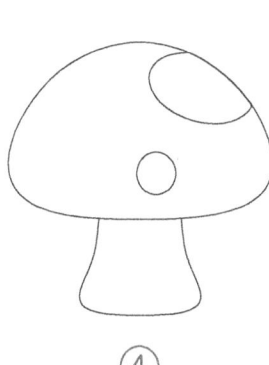

④

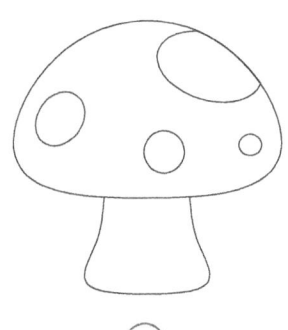

⑤

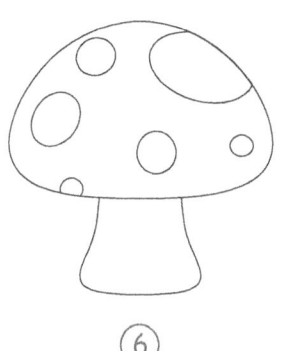

⑥

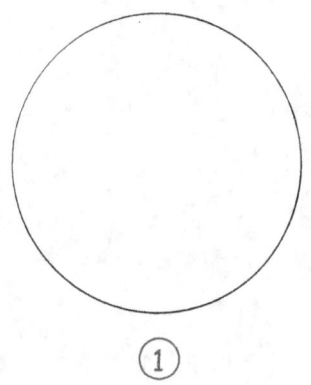

①

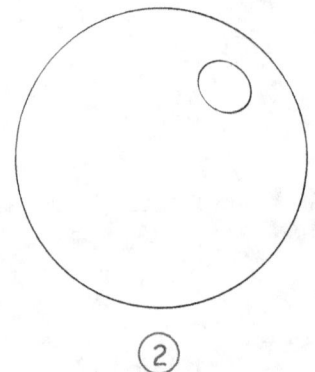

②

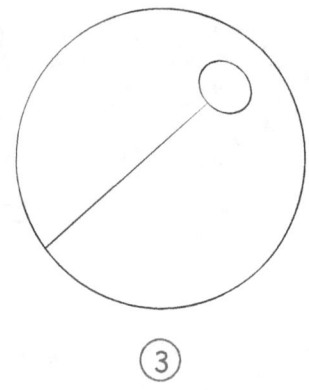

③

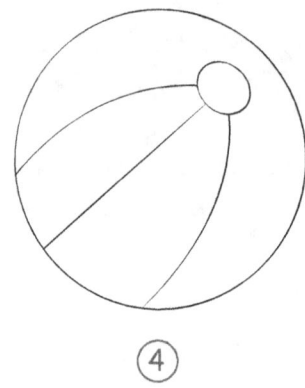

④

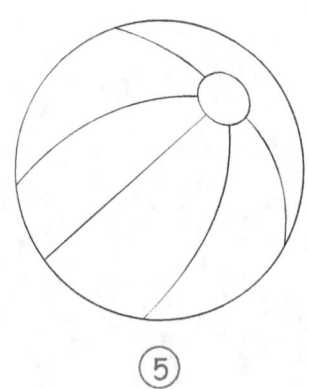

⑤

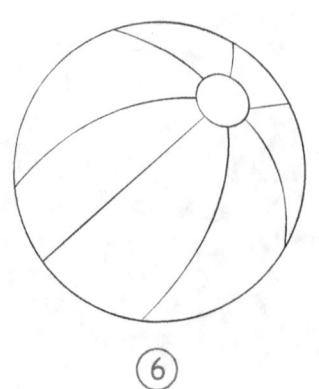

⑥

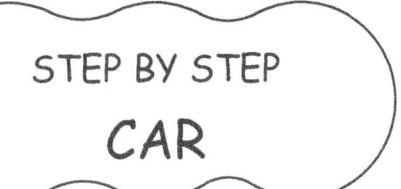

STEP BY STEP
CAR

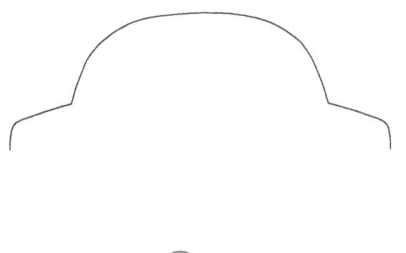

①

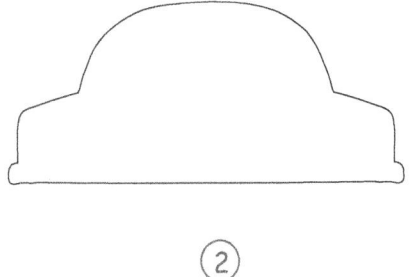

②

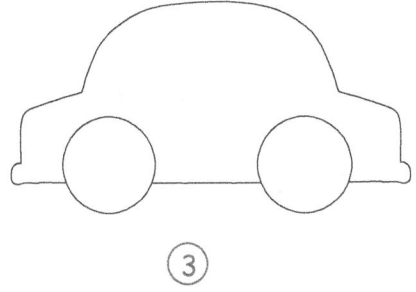

③

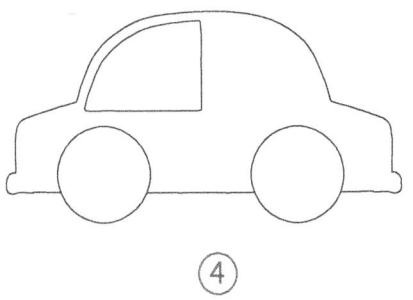

④

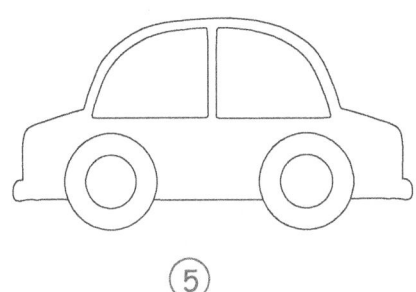

⑤

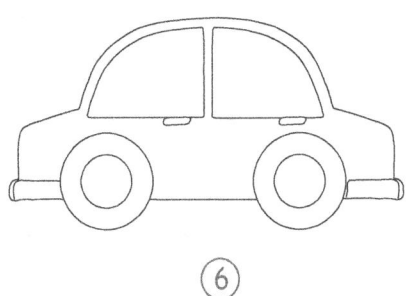

⑥

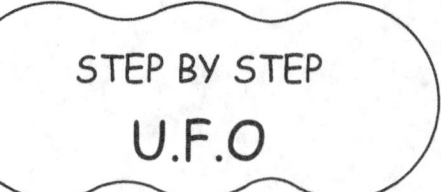

STEP BY STEP
U.F.O

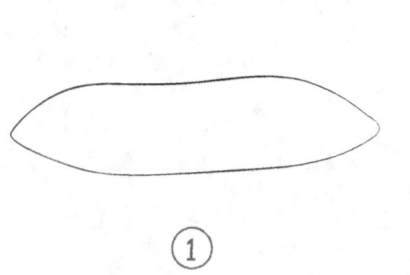

①

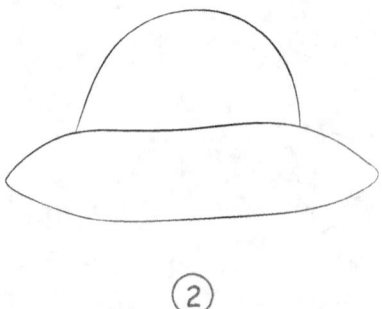

②

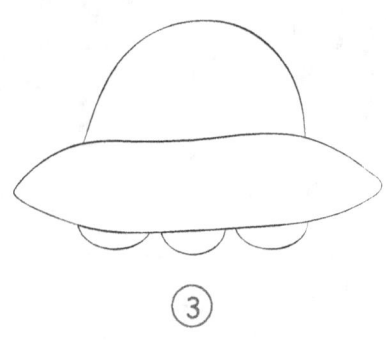

③

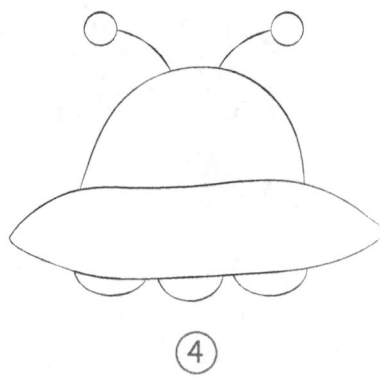

④

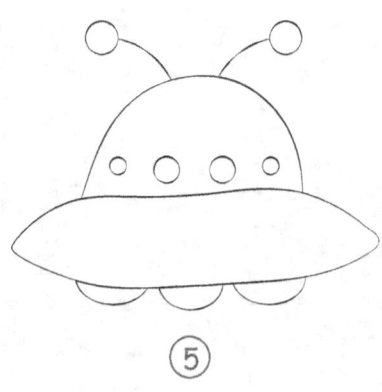

⑤

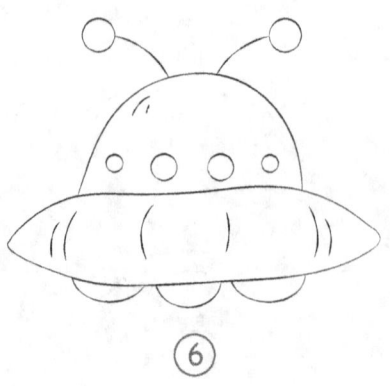

⑥

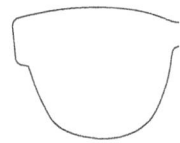

①

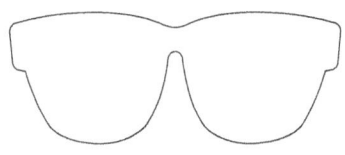

②

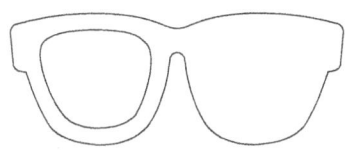

③

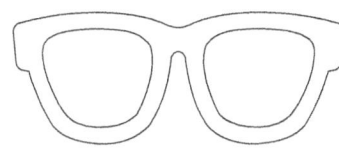

④

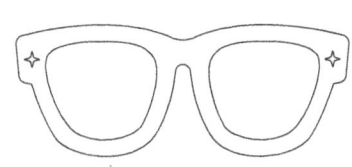

⑤

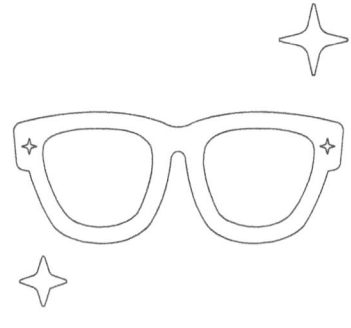

⑥

STEP BY STEP
BEE

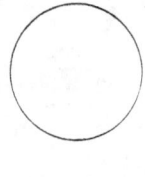

①

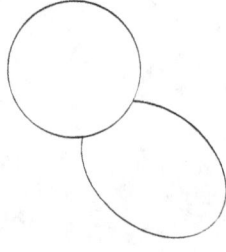

②

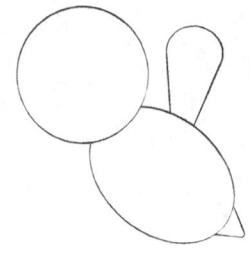

③

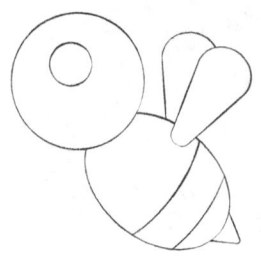

④

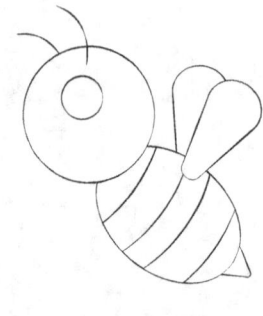

⑤

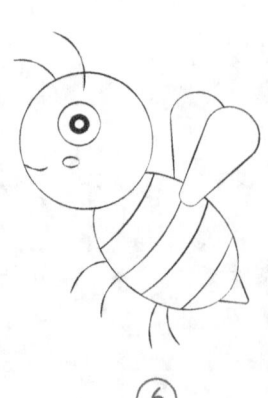

⑥

STEP BY STEP
WATCH

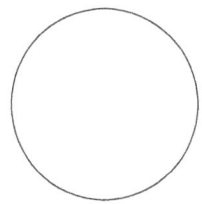

①

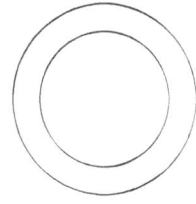

②

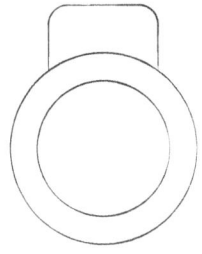

③

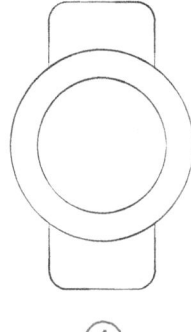

④

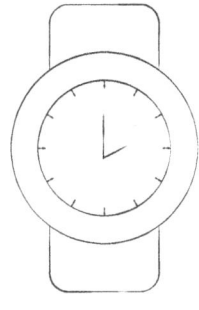

⑤

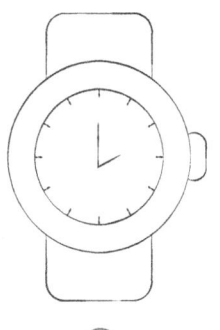

⑥

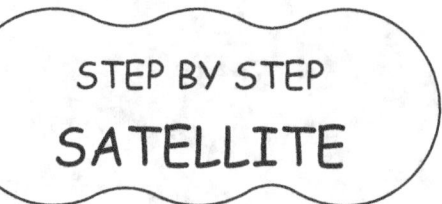

①

②

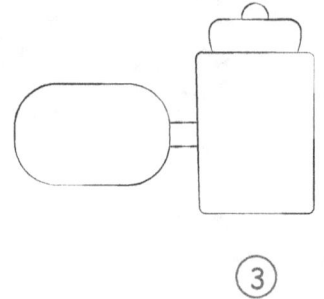

③

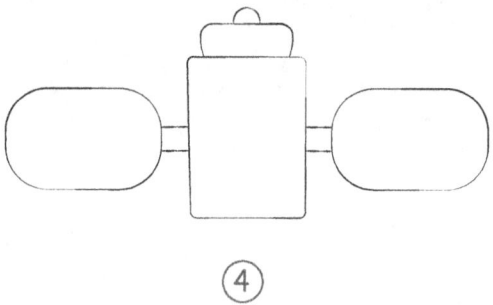

④

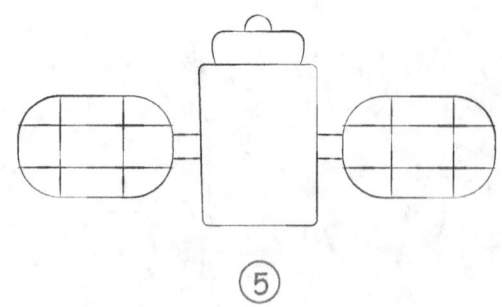

⑤

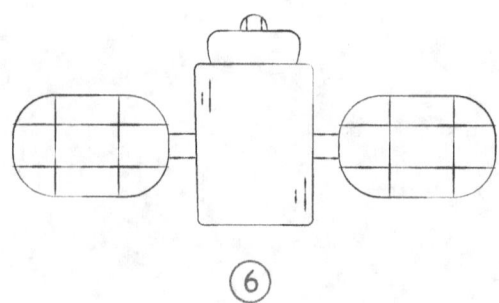

⑥

STEP BY STEP
ICE CREAM

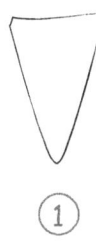

①

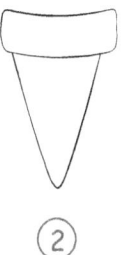

②

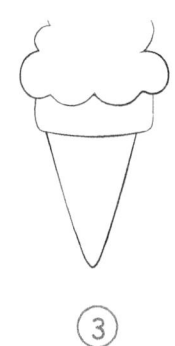

③

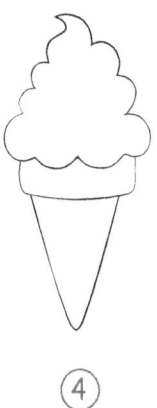

④

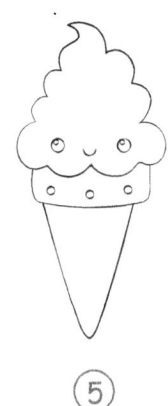

⑤

⑥

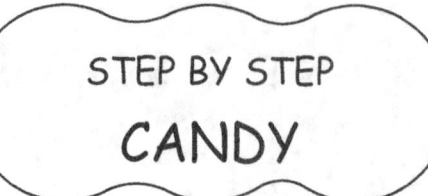

STEP BY STEP
CANDY

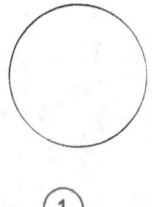

①

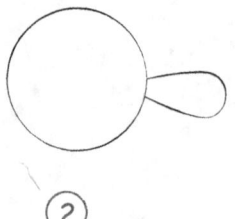

②

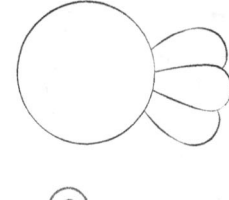

③

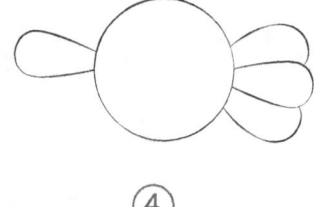

④

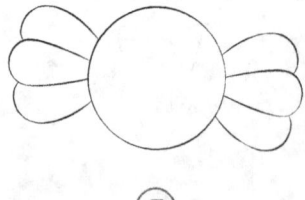

⑤

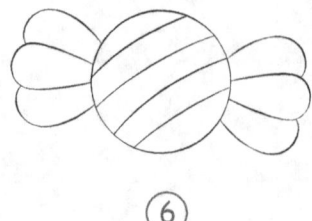

⑥

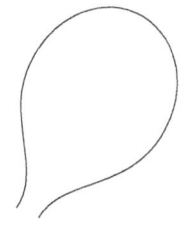

①

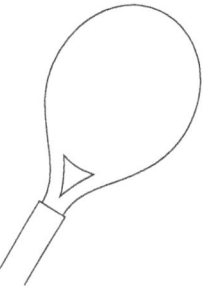

②

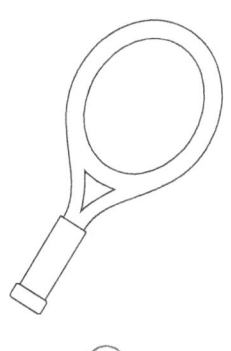

③

④

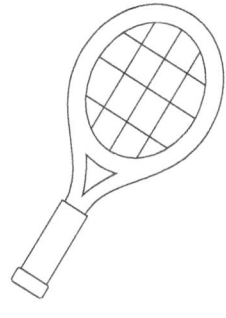

⑤

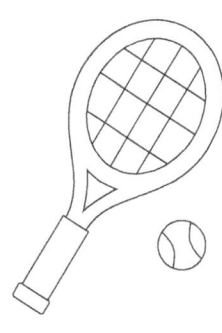

⑥

STEP BY STEP
TOMATO

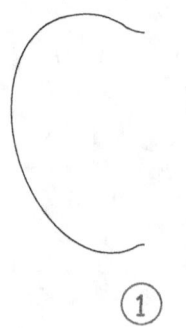

①

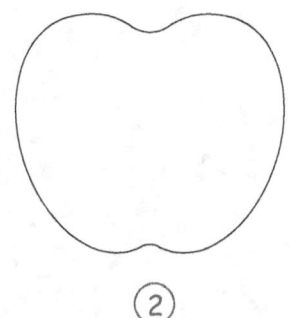

②

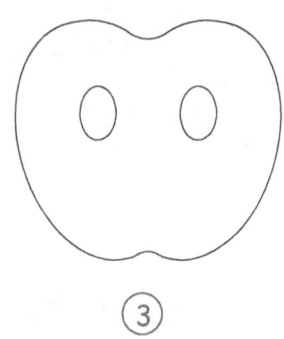

③

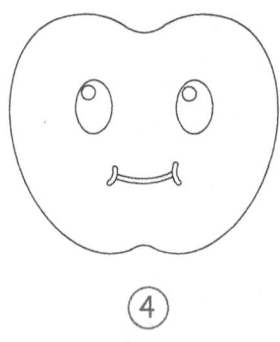

④

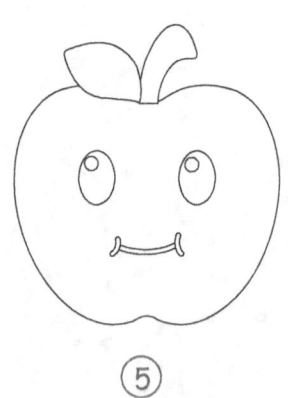

⑤

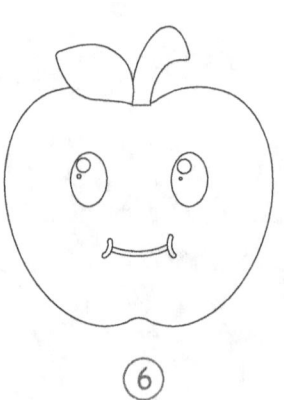

⑥

STEP BY STEP
TANGERINE

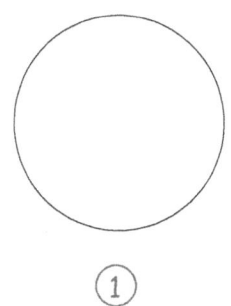

①

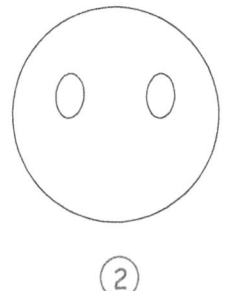

②

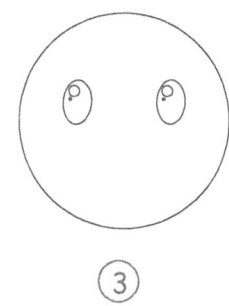

③

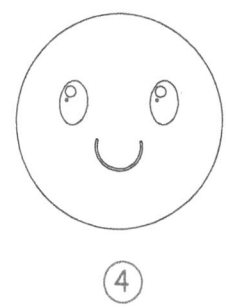

④

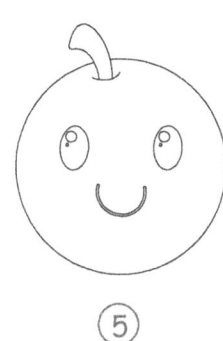

⑤

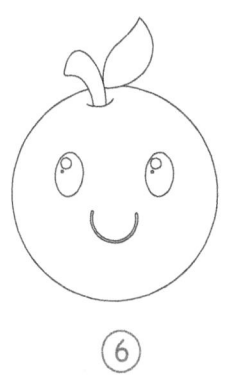

⑥

STEP BY STEP
LEMON

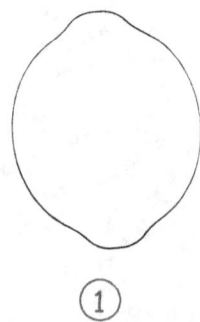

①

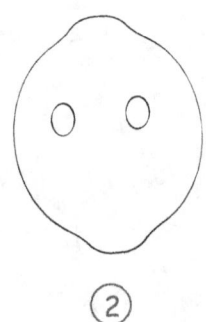

②

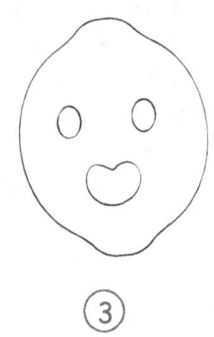

③

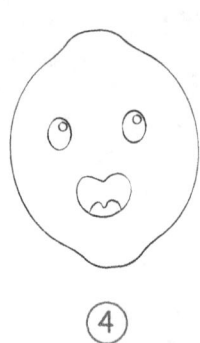

④

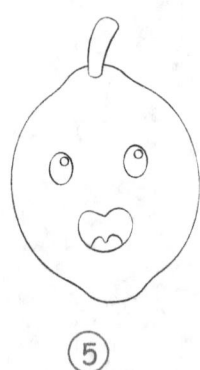

⑤

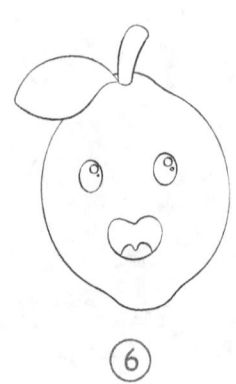

⑥

STEP BY STEP
STRAWBERRY

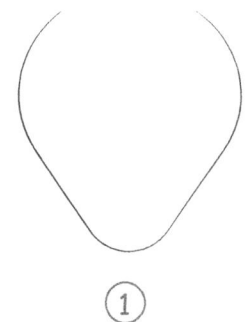

①

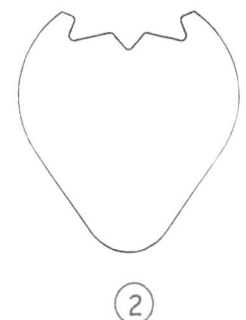

②

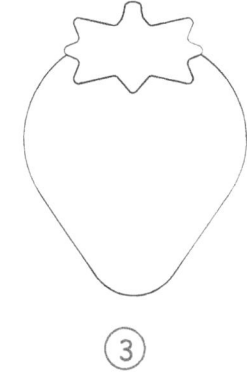

③

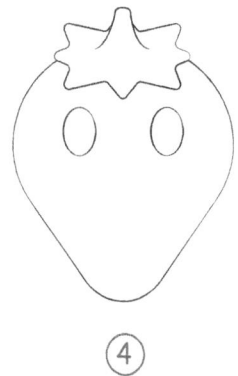

④

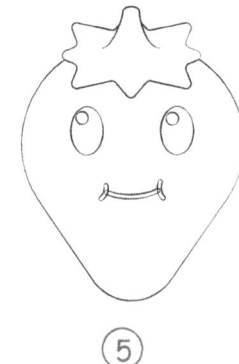

⑤

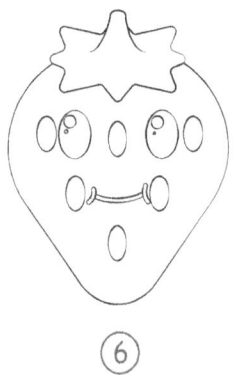

⑥

①

②

③

④

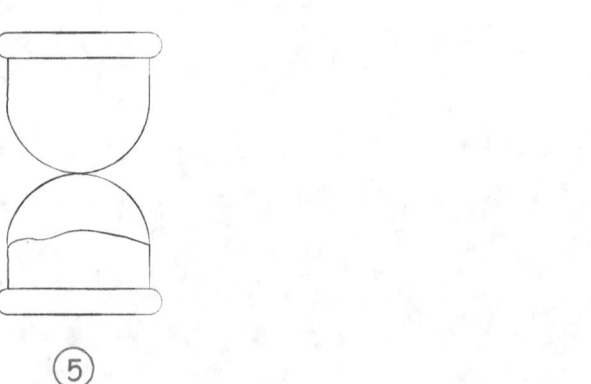

⑤

⑥

STEP BY STEP
CHERRY

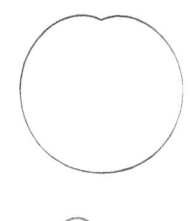

①

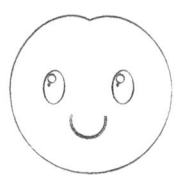

②

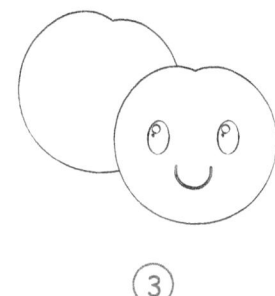

③

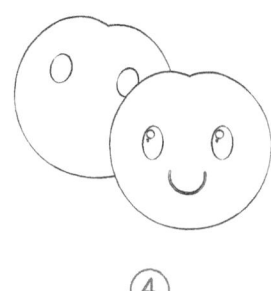

④

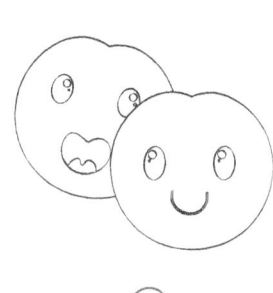

⑤

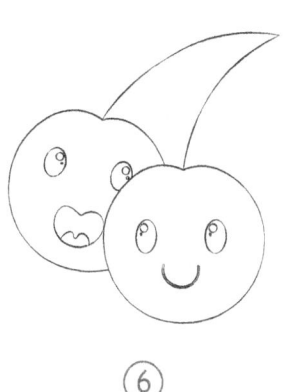

⑥

STEP BY STEP
BASKETBALL

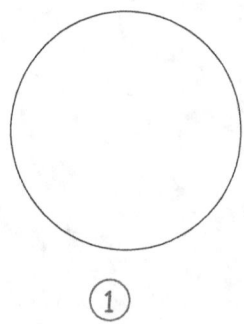

①

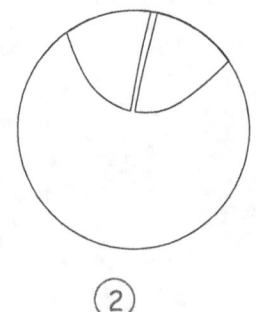

②

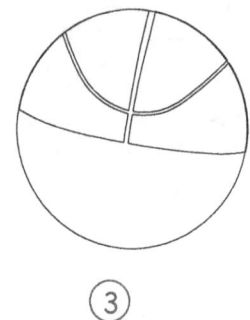

③

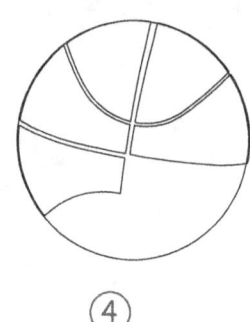

④

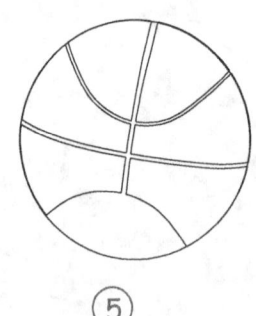

⑤

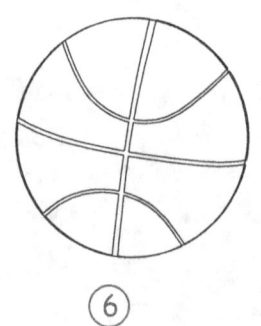

⑥

STEP BY STEP
ROCKET

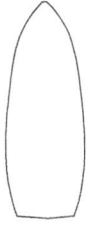

①

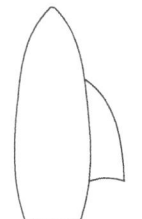

②

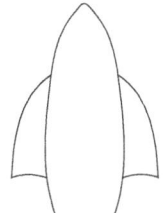

③

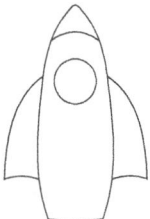

④

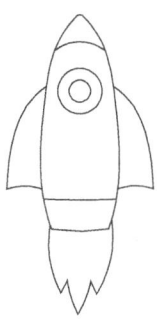

⑤

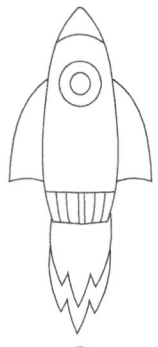

⑥

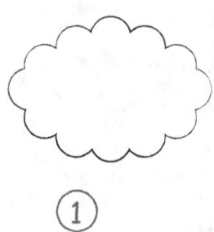

①

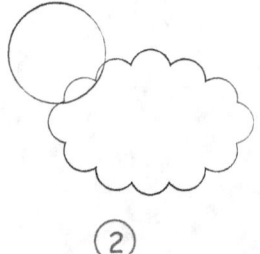

②

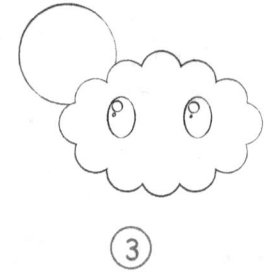

③

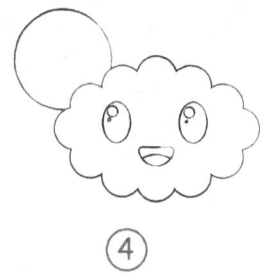

④

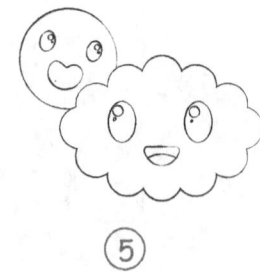

⑤

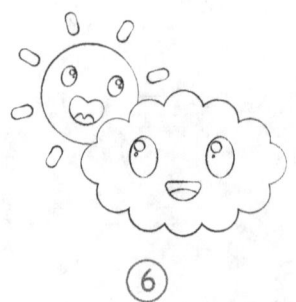

⑥

STEP BY STEP
TELESCOPE

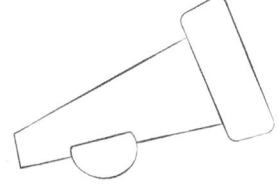

①

②

③

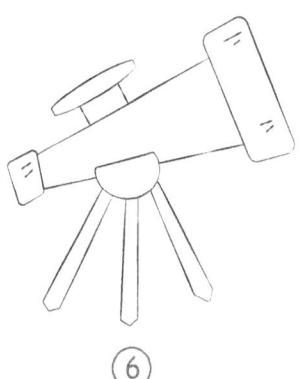

④

⑤

⑥

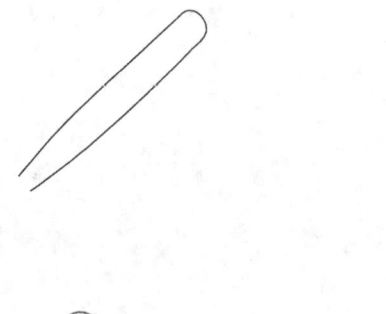

①

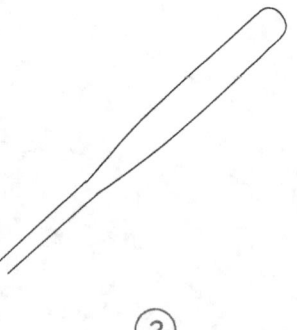

②

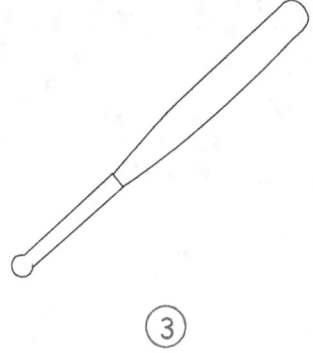

③

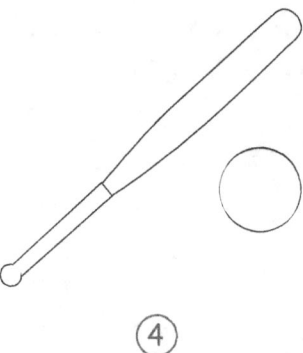

④

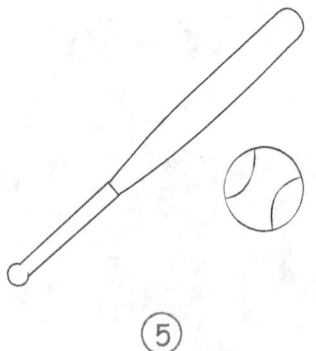

⑤

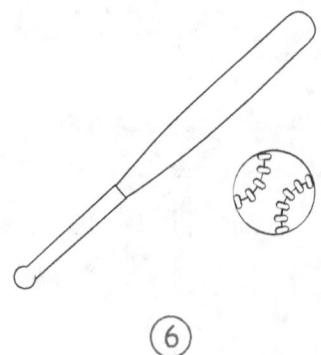

⑥

STEP BY STEP
HORSE

①

②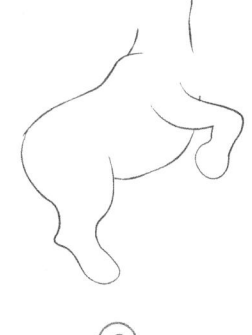

③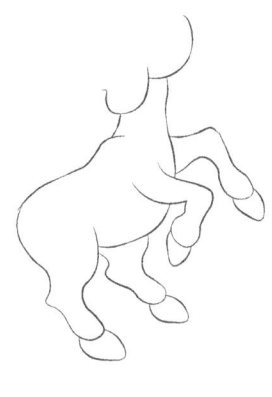

④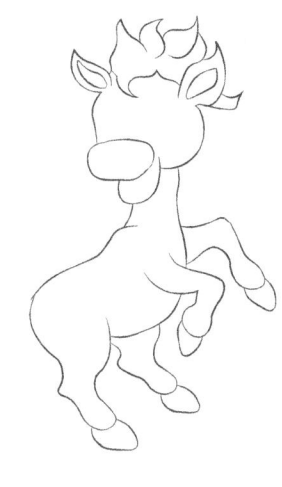

⑤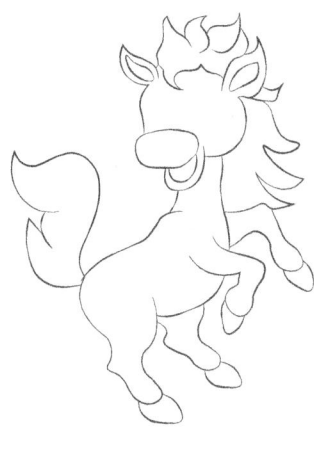

⑥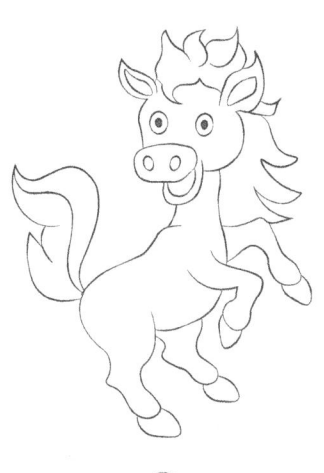

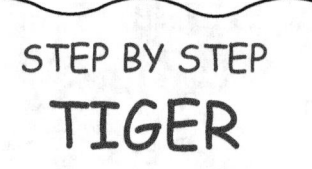

STEP BY STEP
TIGER

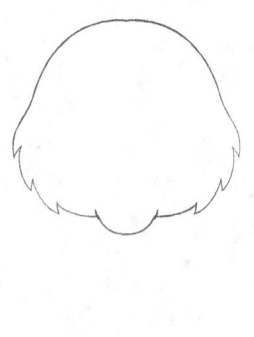

①

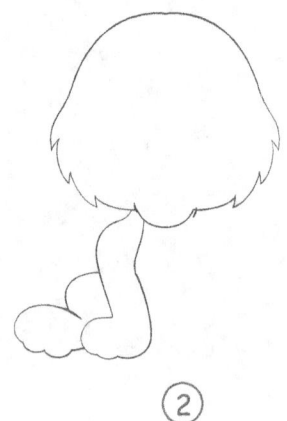

②

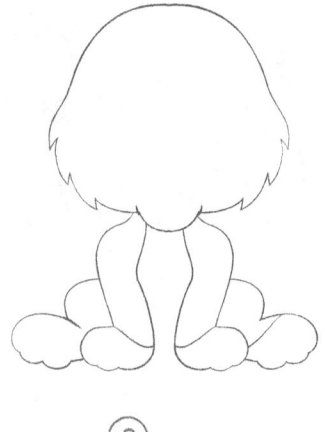

③

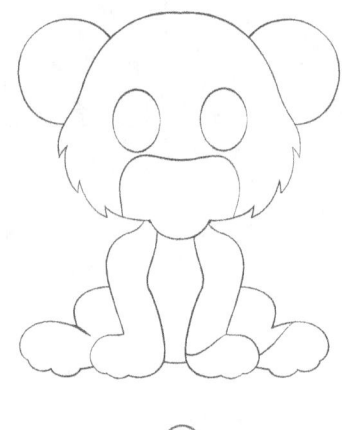

④

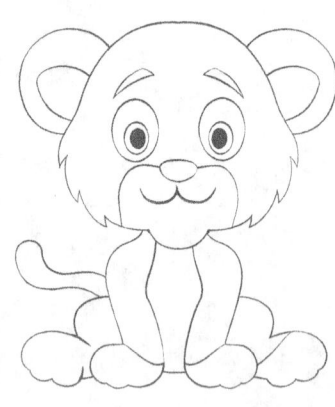

⑤

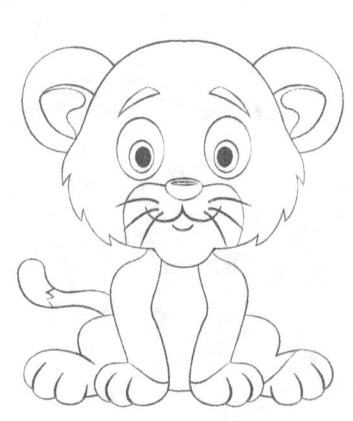

⑥

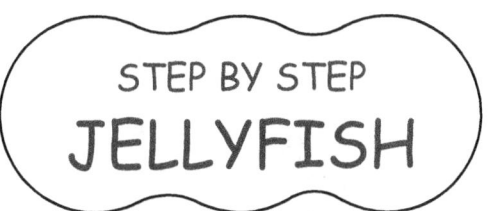

STEP BY STEP
JELLYFISH

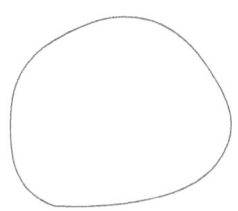

①

②

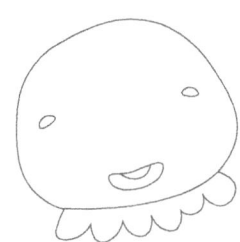

③

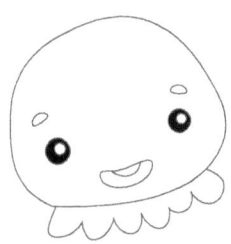

④

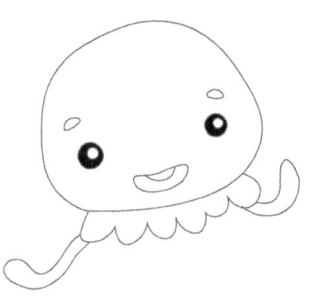

⑤

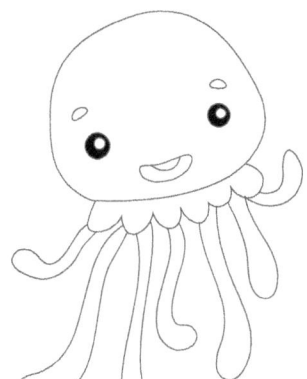

⑥

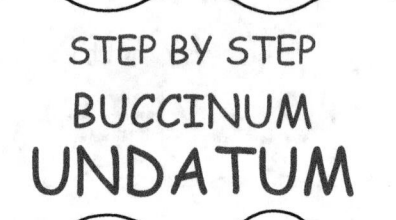

STEP BY STEP
BUCCINUM
UNDATUM

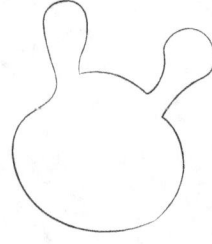

①

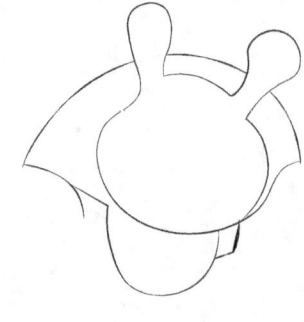

②

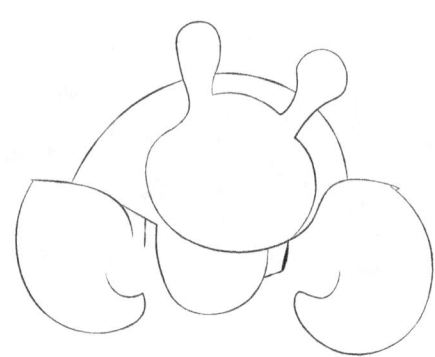

③

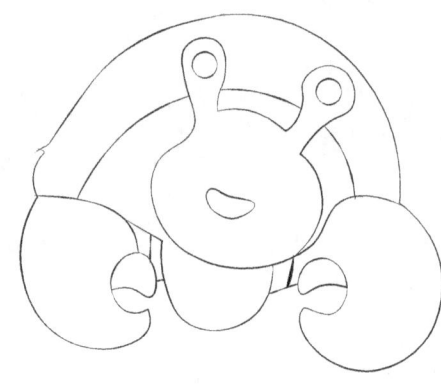

④

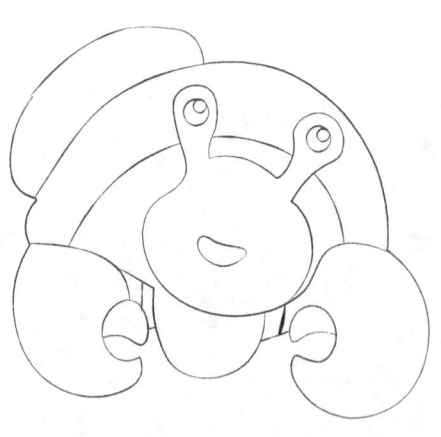

⑤

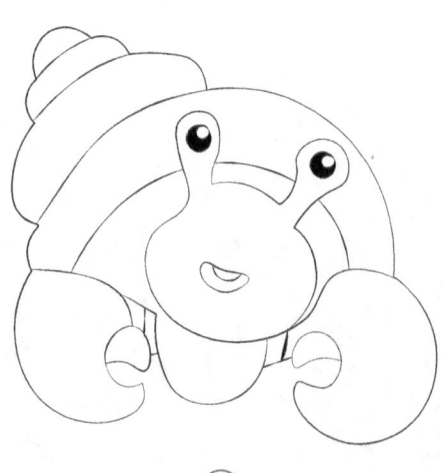

⑥

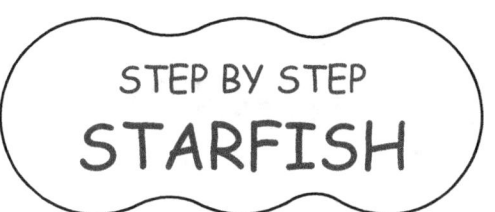

STEP BY STEP
STARFISH

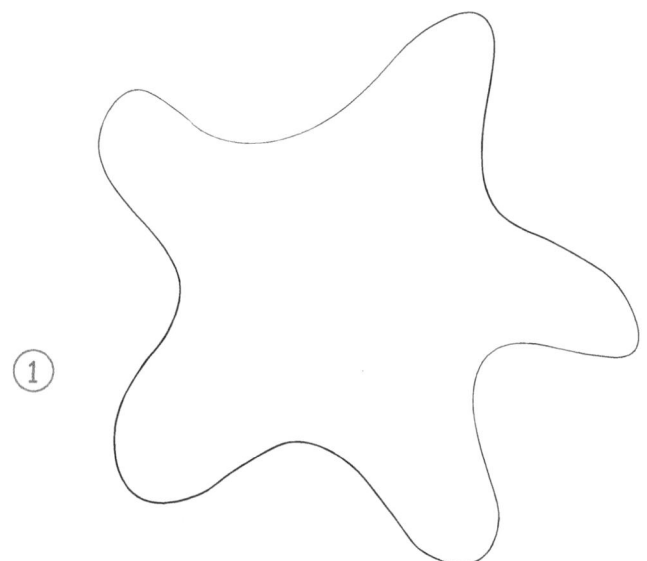

①

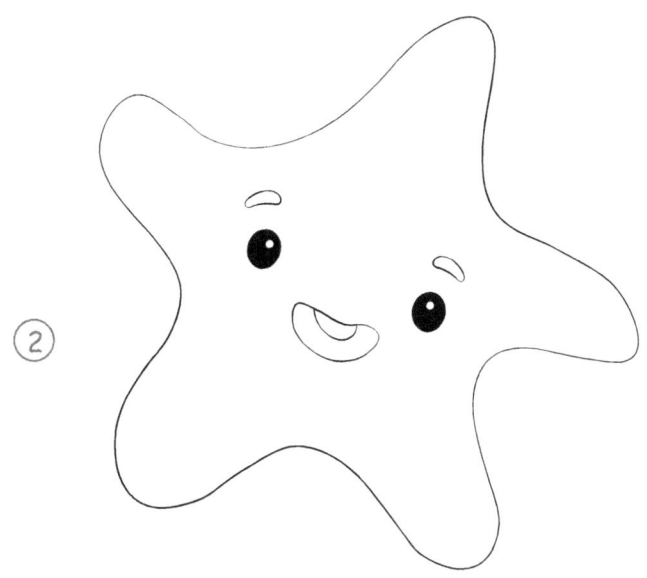

②

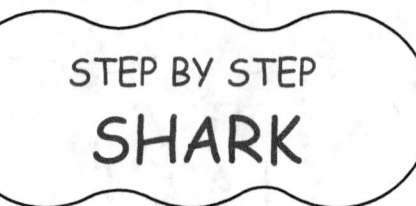

STEP BY STEP
SHARK

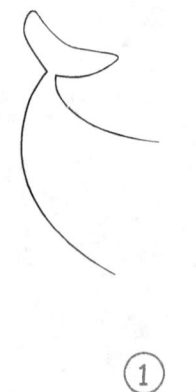

①

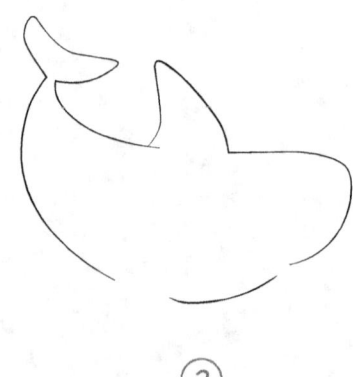

②

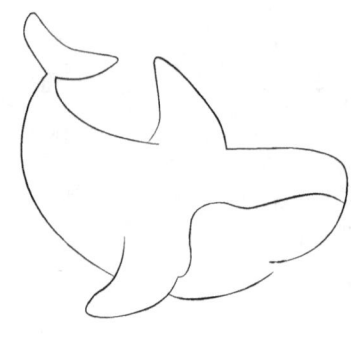

③

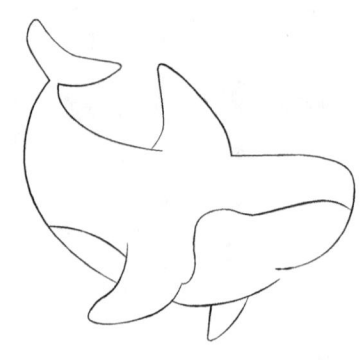

④

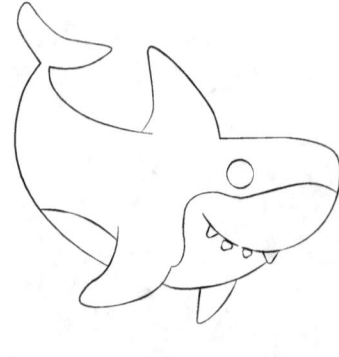

⑤

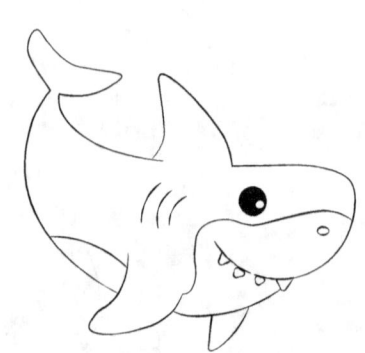

⑥

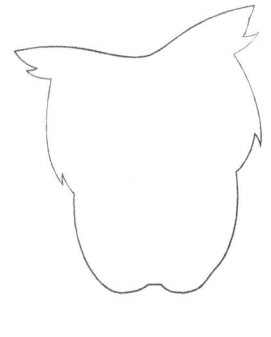

①

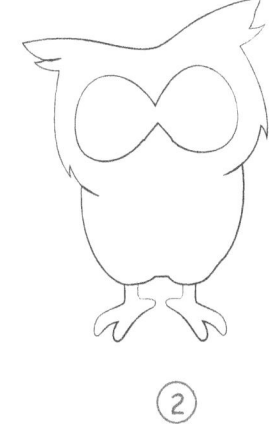

②

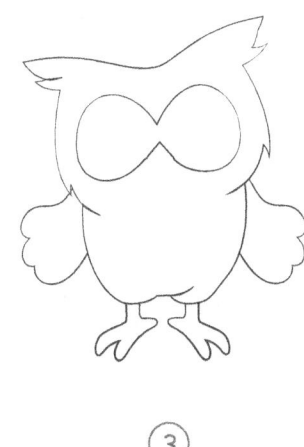

③

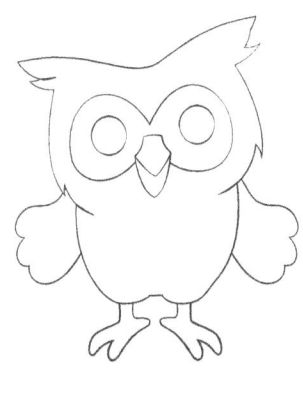

④

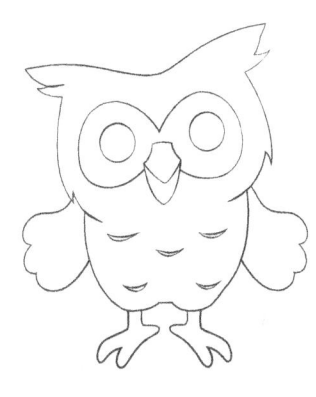

⑤

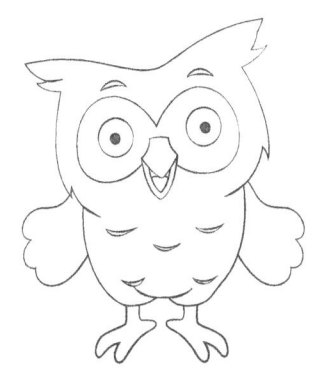

⑥

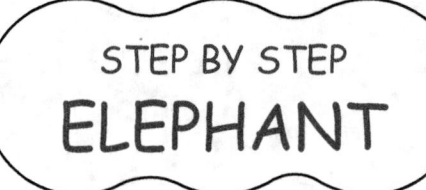

STEP BY STEP
ELEPHANT

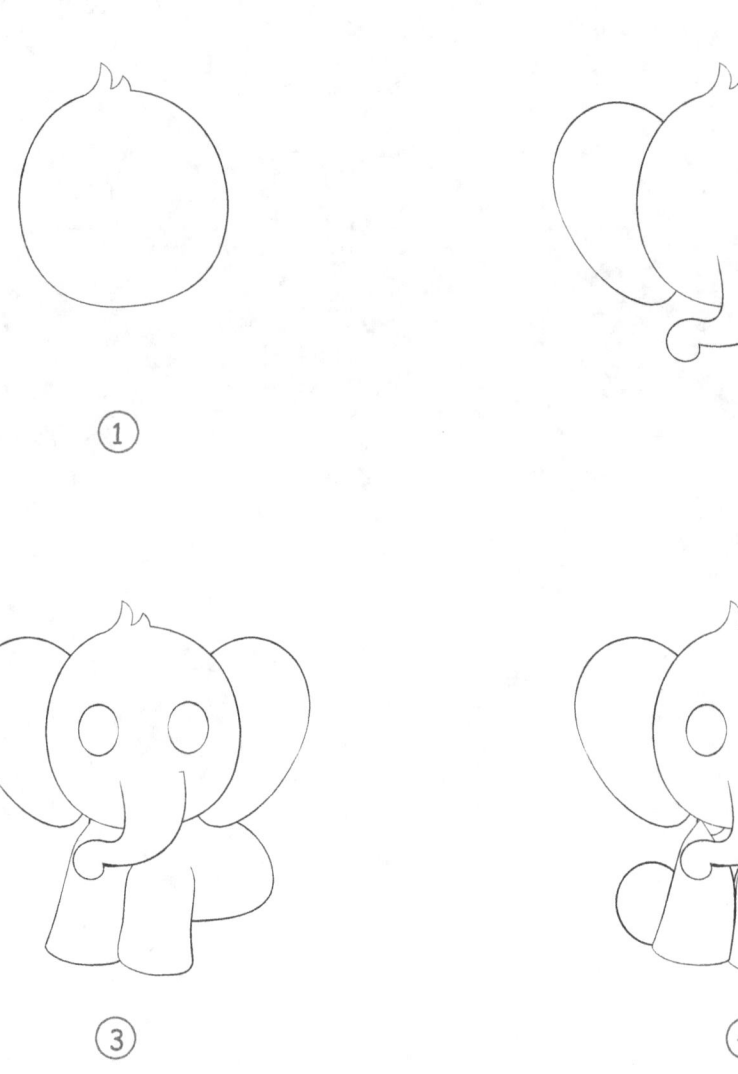

① ②

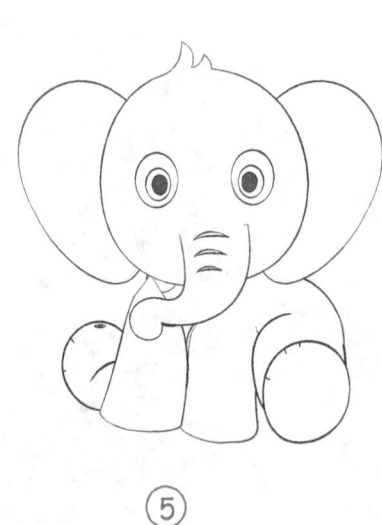

③ ④

⑤ ⑥

STEP BY STEP
CAT

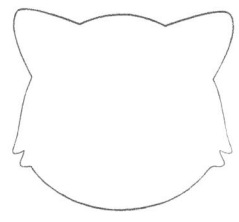

①

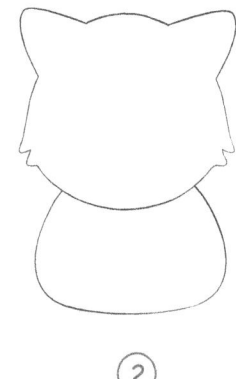

②

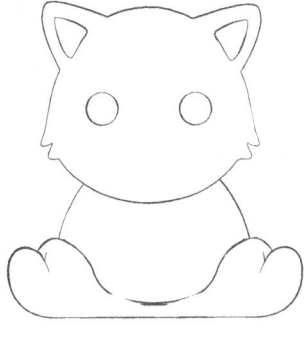

③

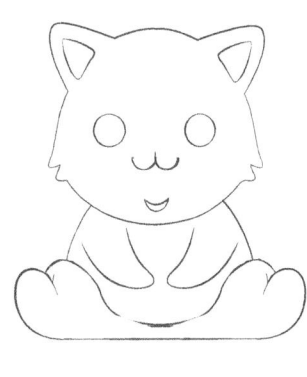

④

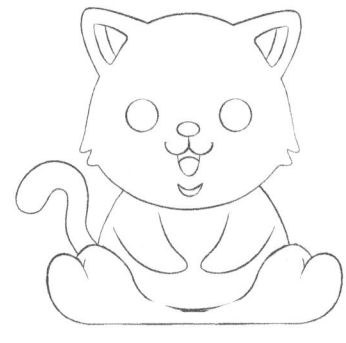

⑤

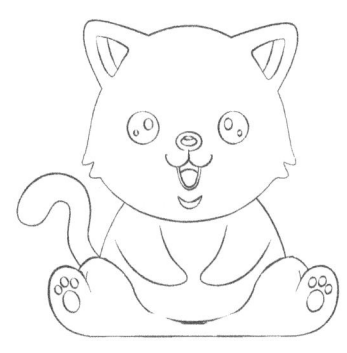

⑥

STEP BY STEP
OCTOPUS

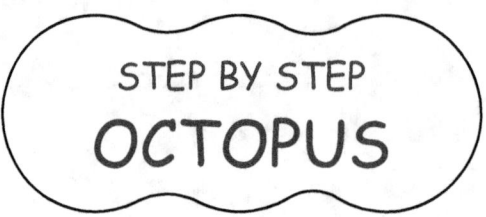

① ②

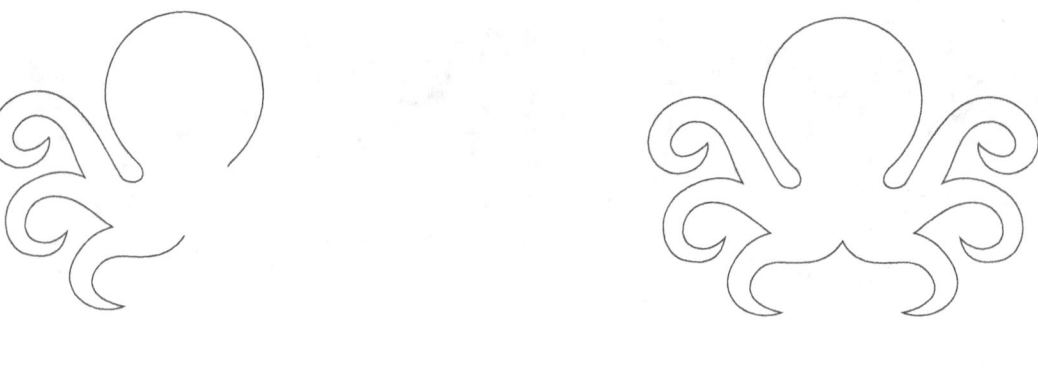

③ ④

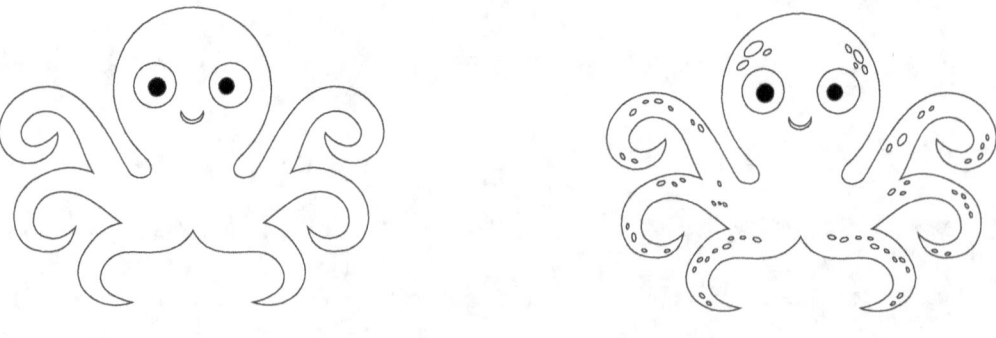

⑤ ⑥

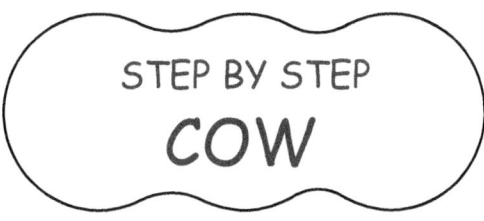

STEP BY STEP
COW

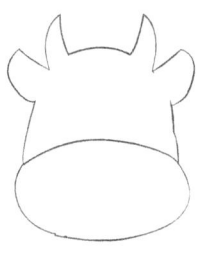

①

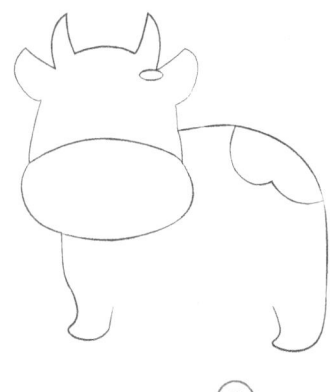

②

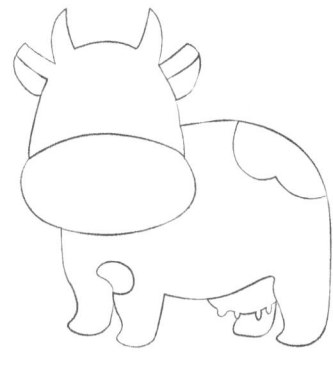

③

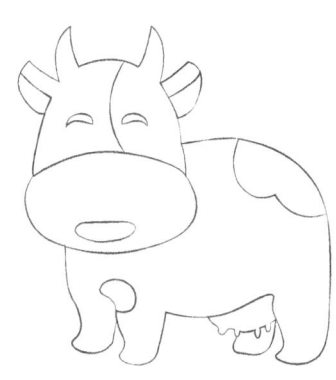

④

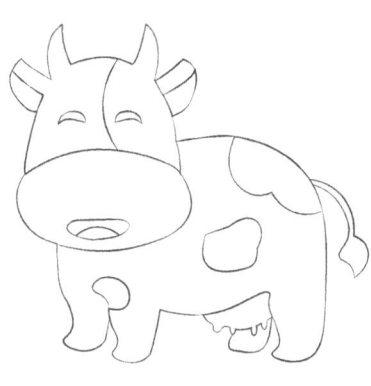

⑤

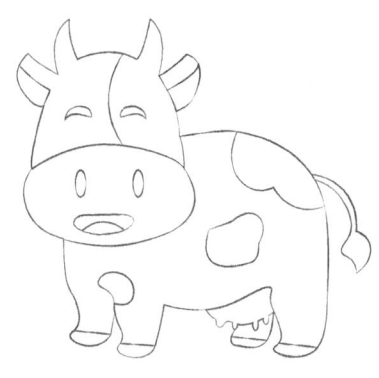

⑥

STEP BY STEP
FOX

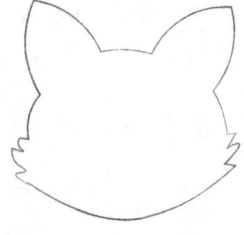

①

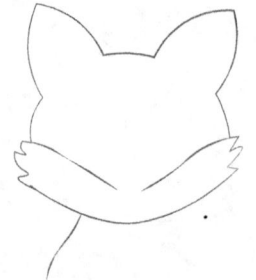

②

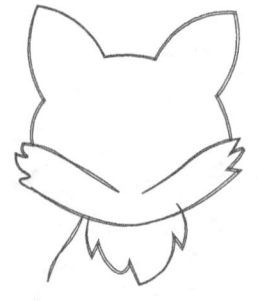

③

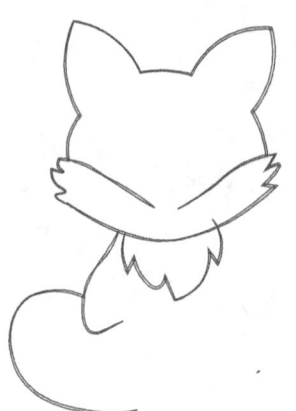

④

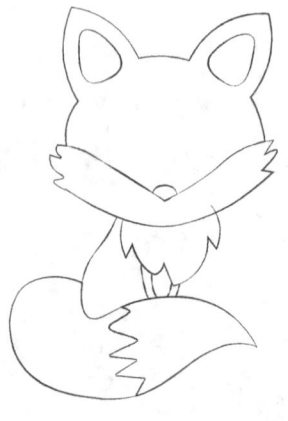

⑤

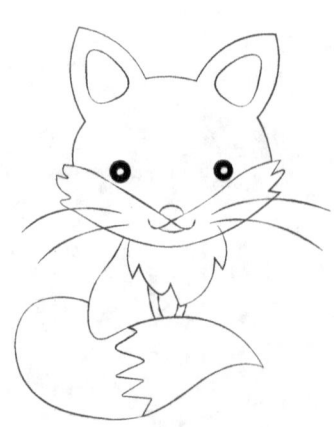

⑥

STEP BY STEP
PIG

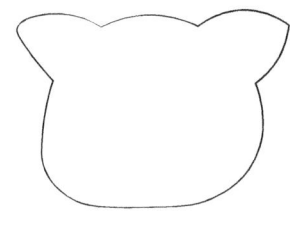

①

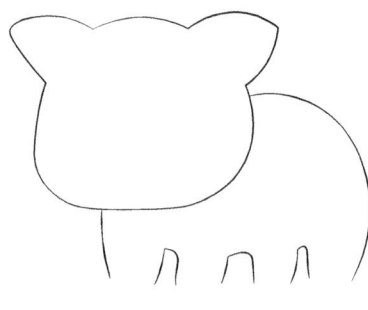

②

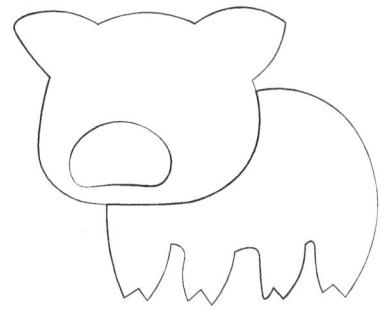

③

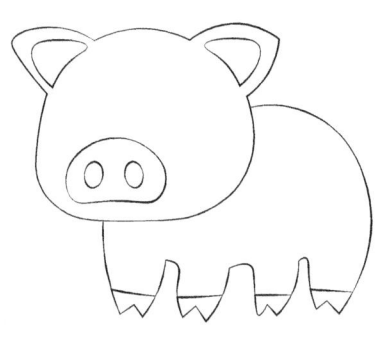

④

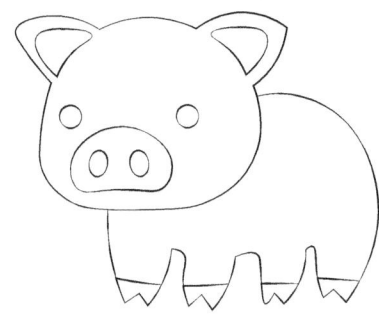

⑤

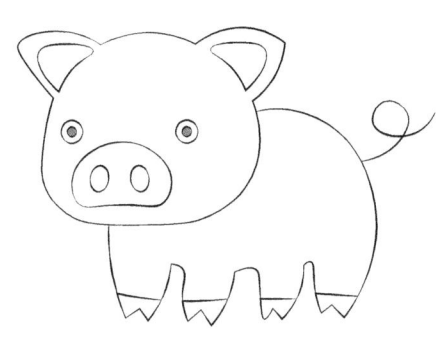

⑥

STEP BY STEP
FROG

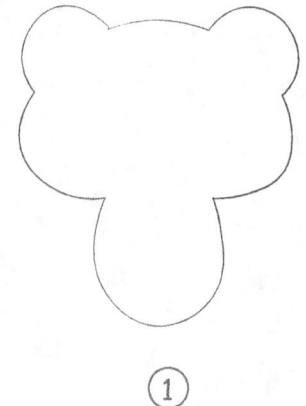

①

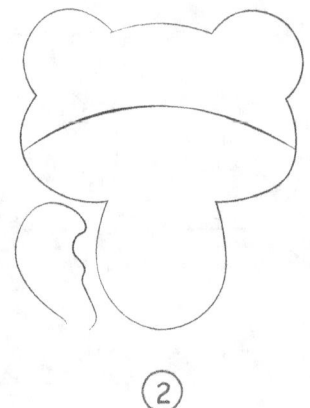

②

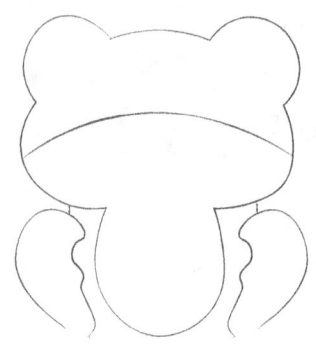

③

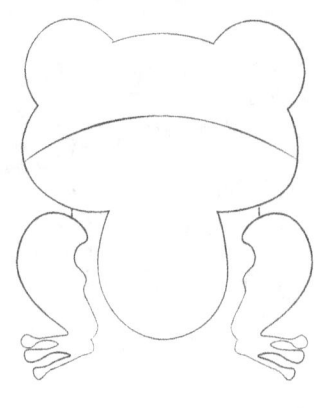

④

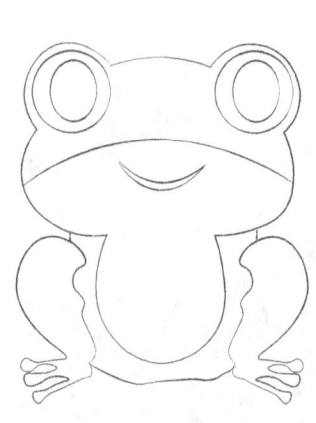

⑤

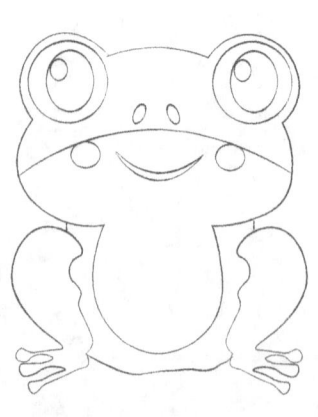

⑥

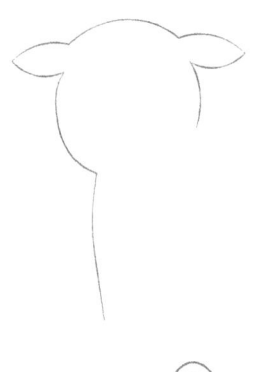

①

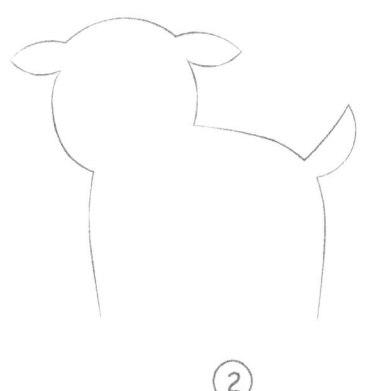

②

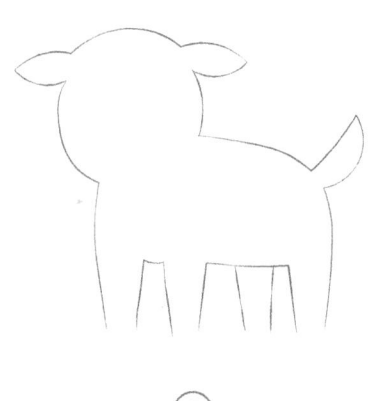

③

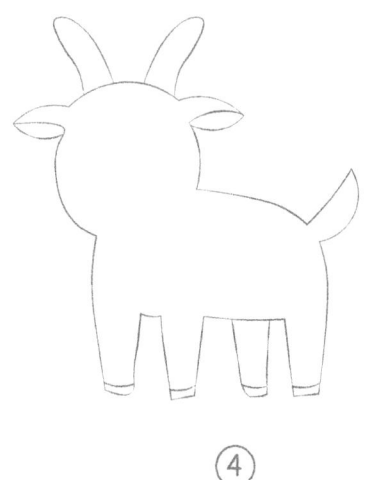

④

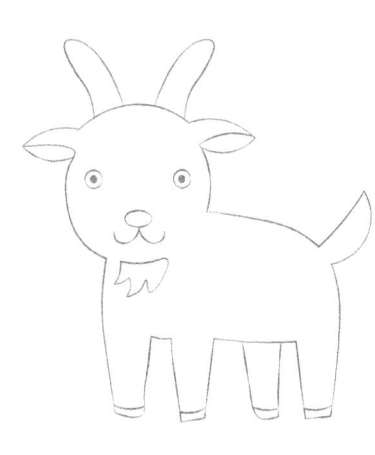

⑤

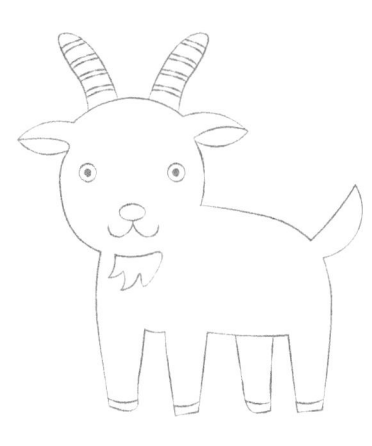

⑥

STEP BY STEP
PANDA

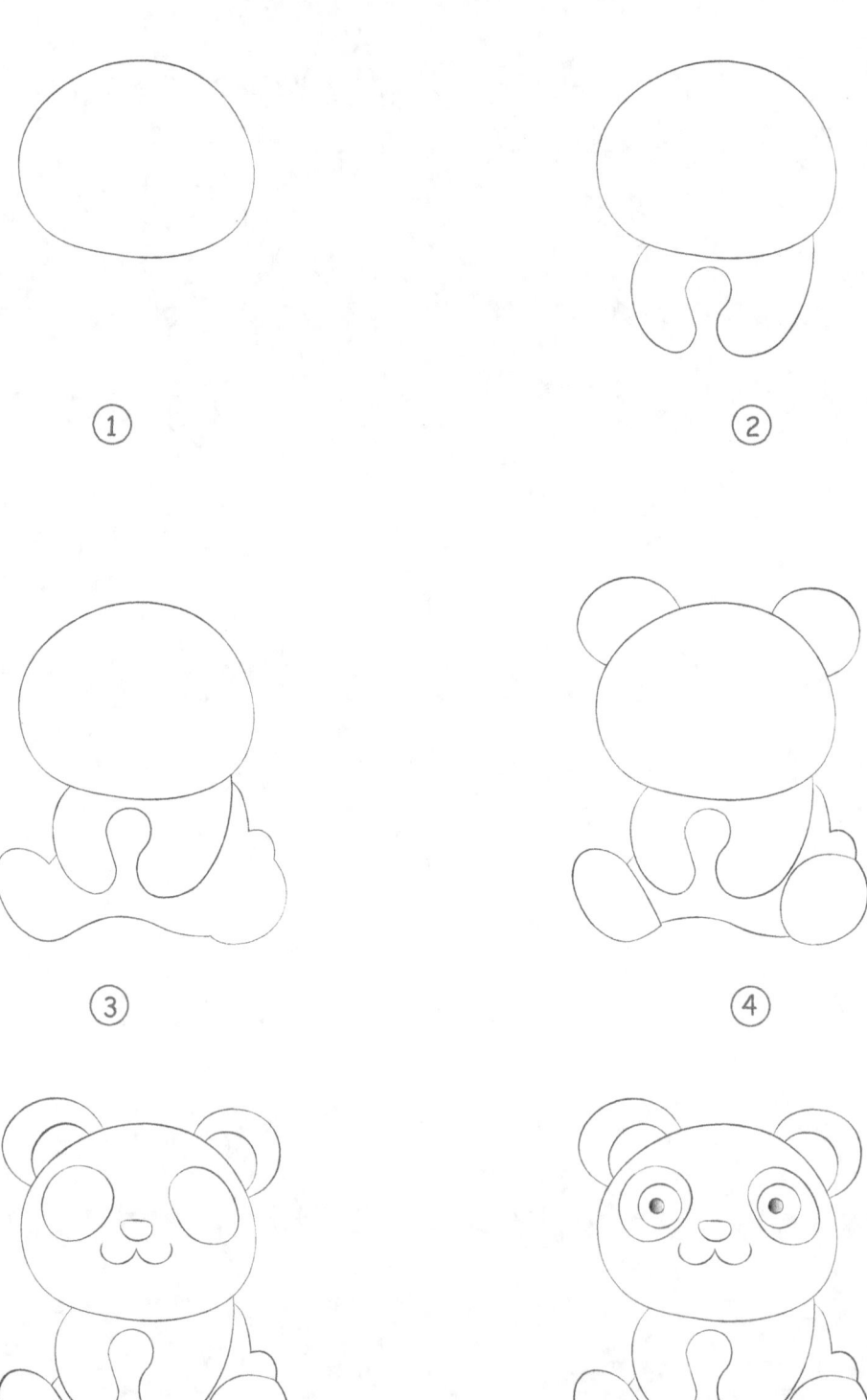

STEP BY STEP
RAT

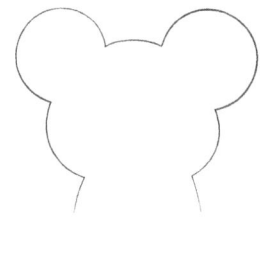

①

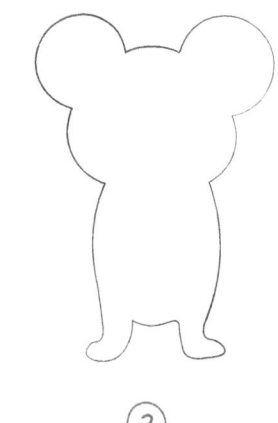

②

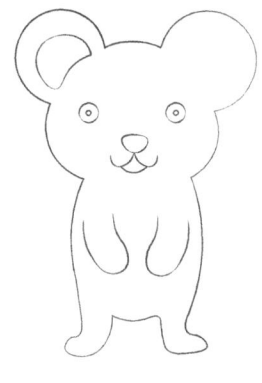

③

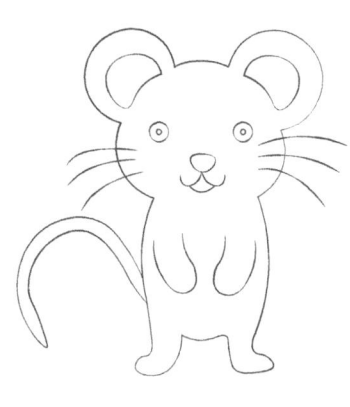

④

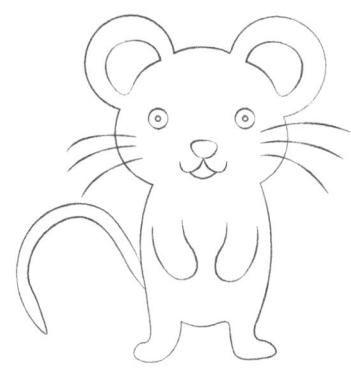

⑤

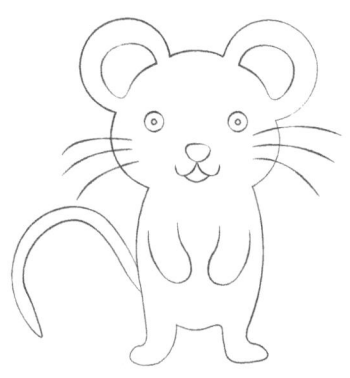

⑥

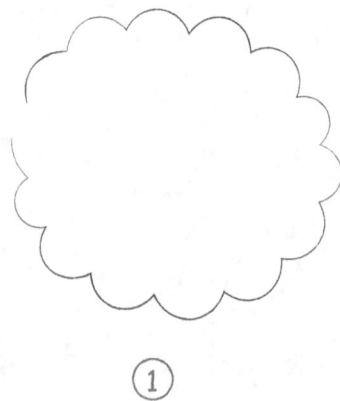

①

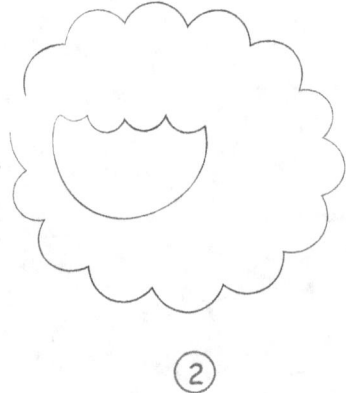

②

③

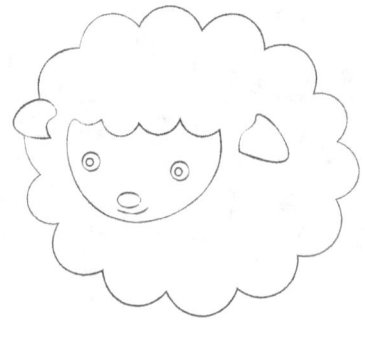

④

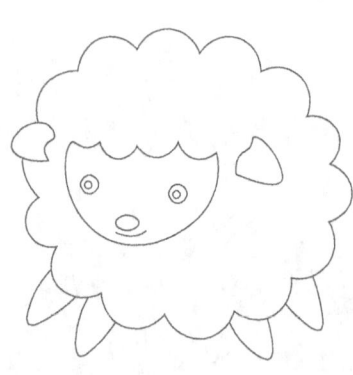

⑤

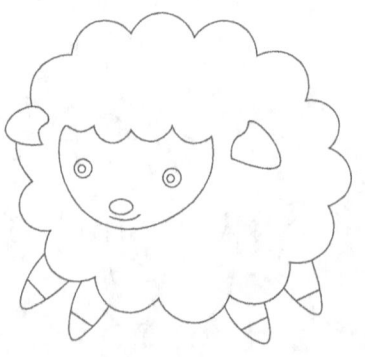

⑥

STEP BY STEP
DOG

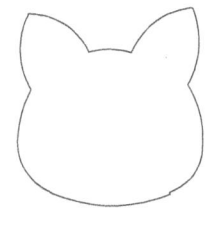

①

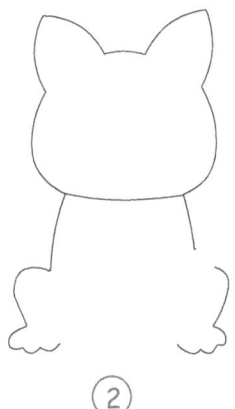

②

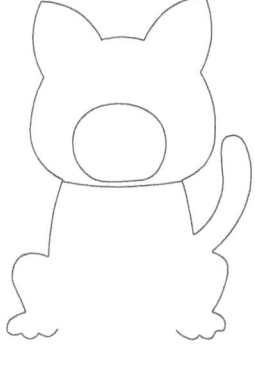

③

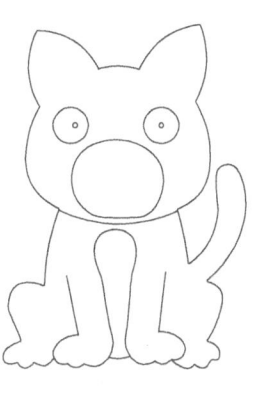

④

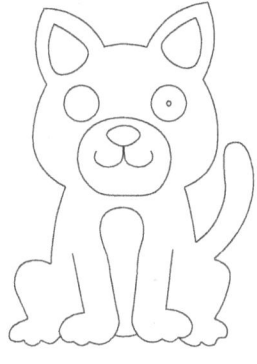

⑤

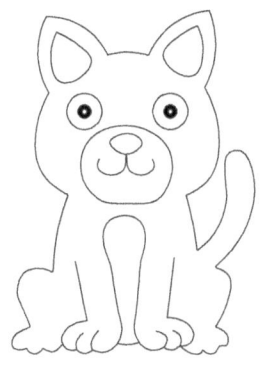

⑥

STEP BY STEP
KANGAROO

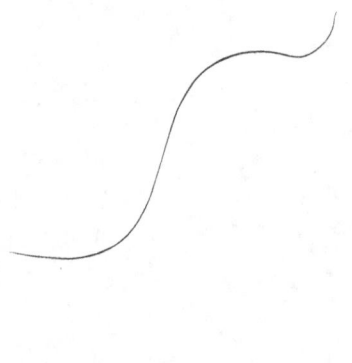

①

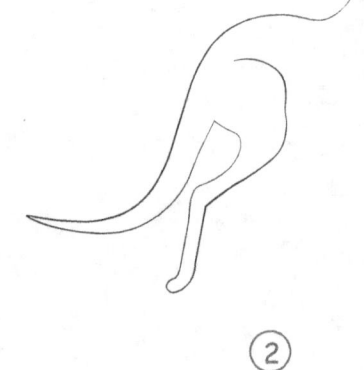

②

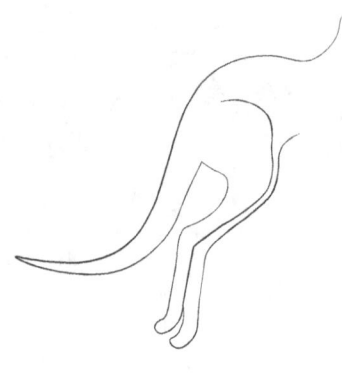

③

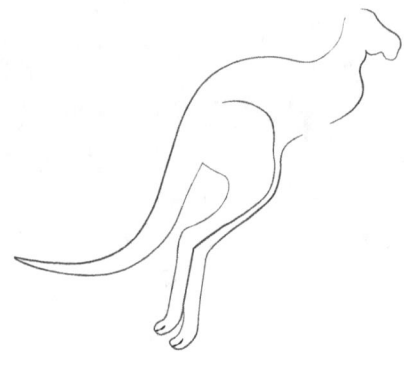

④

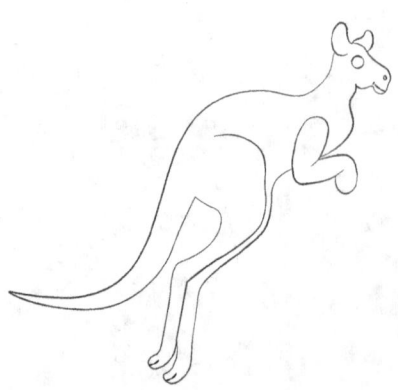

⑤

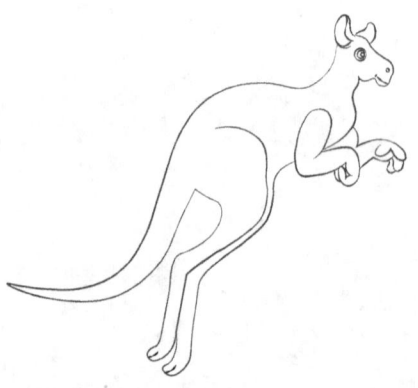

⑥

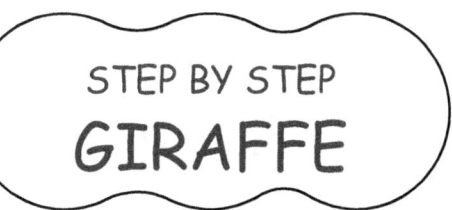

STEP BY STEP
GIRAFFE

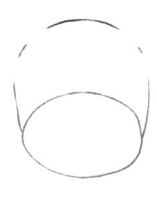

①

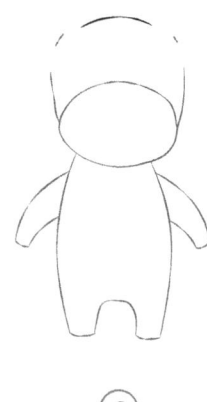

②

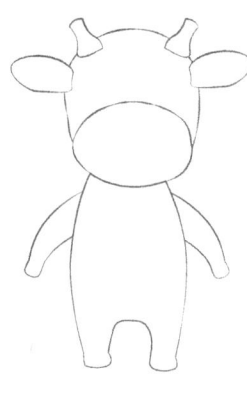

③

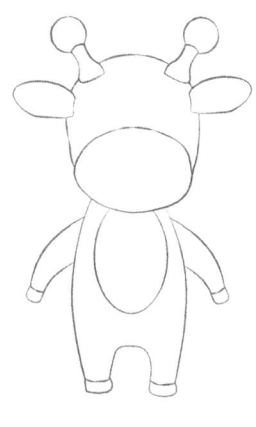

④

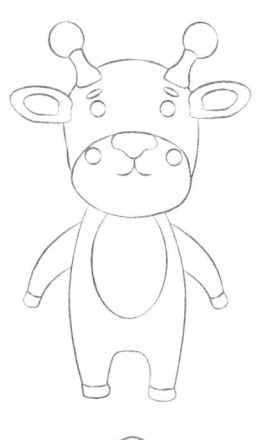

⑤

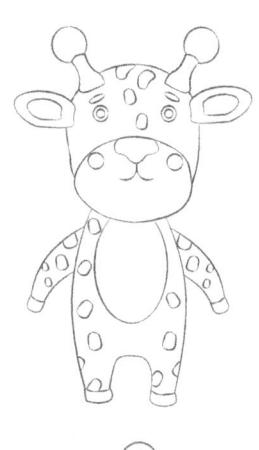

⑥

STEP BY STEP
LION

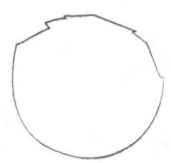

①

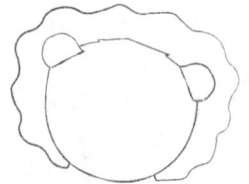

②

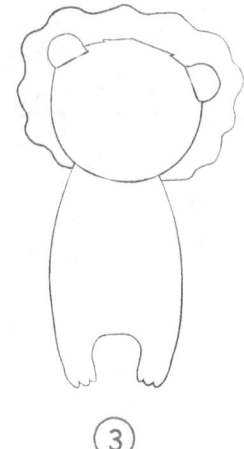

③

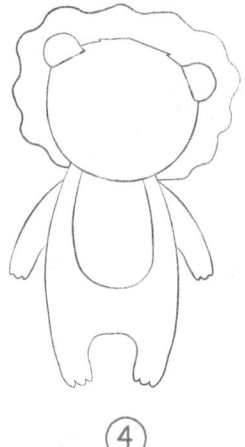

④

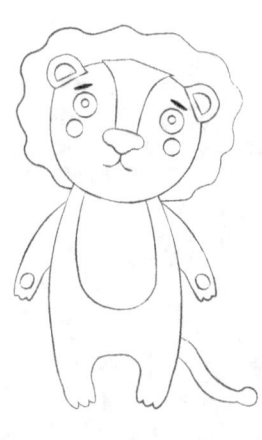

⑤

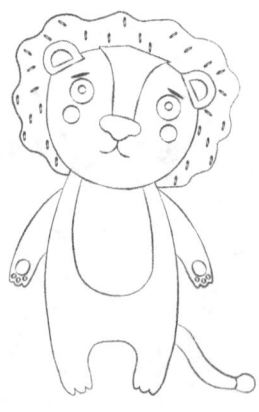

⑥

STEP BY STEP
CAT

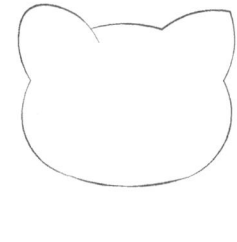

①

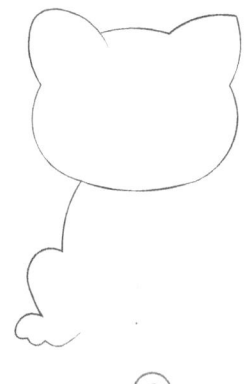

②

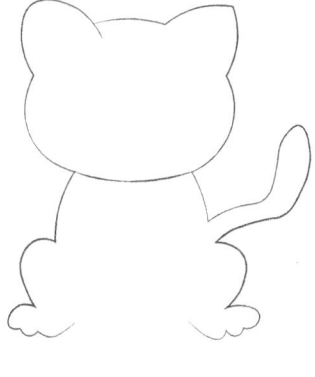

③

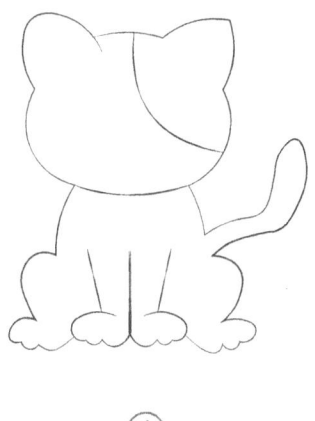

④

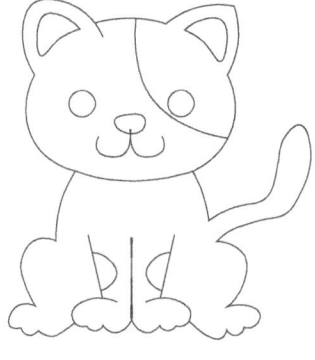

⑤

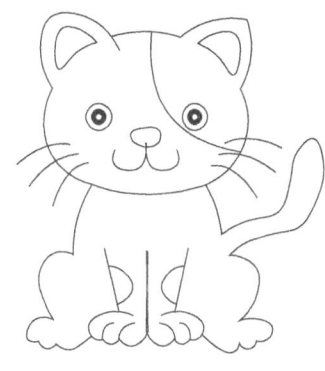

⑥

STEP BY STEP
PTEROSAUR

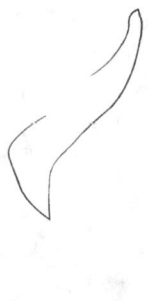

①

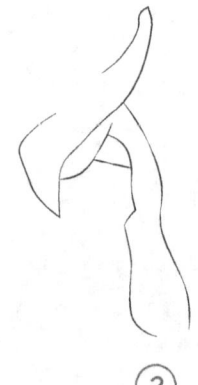

②

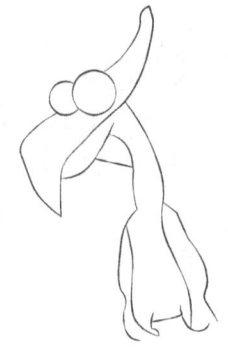

③

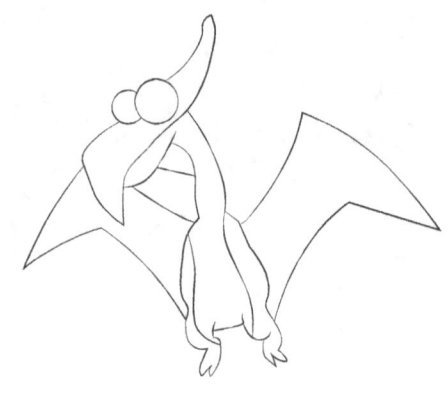

④

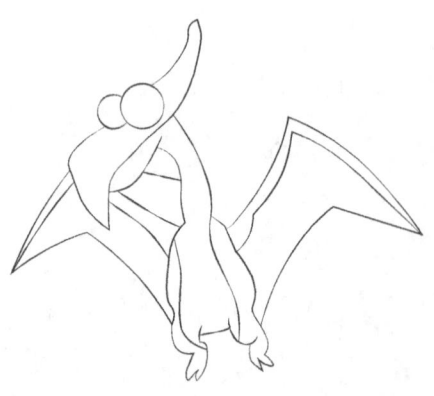

⑤

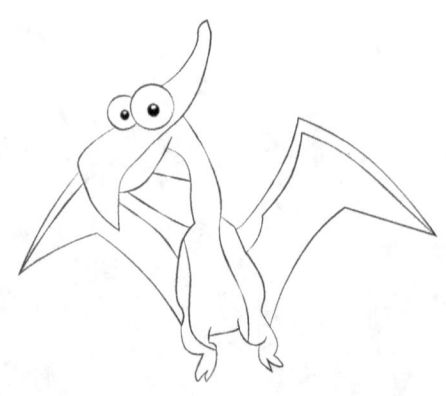

⑥

STEP BY STEP
BRACHIOSAURUS

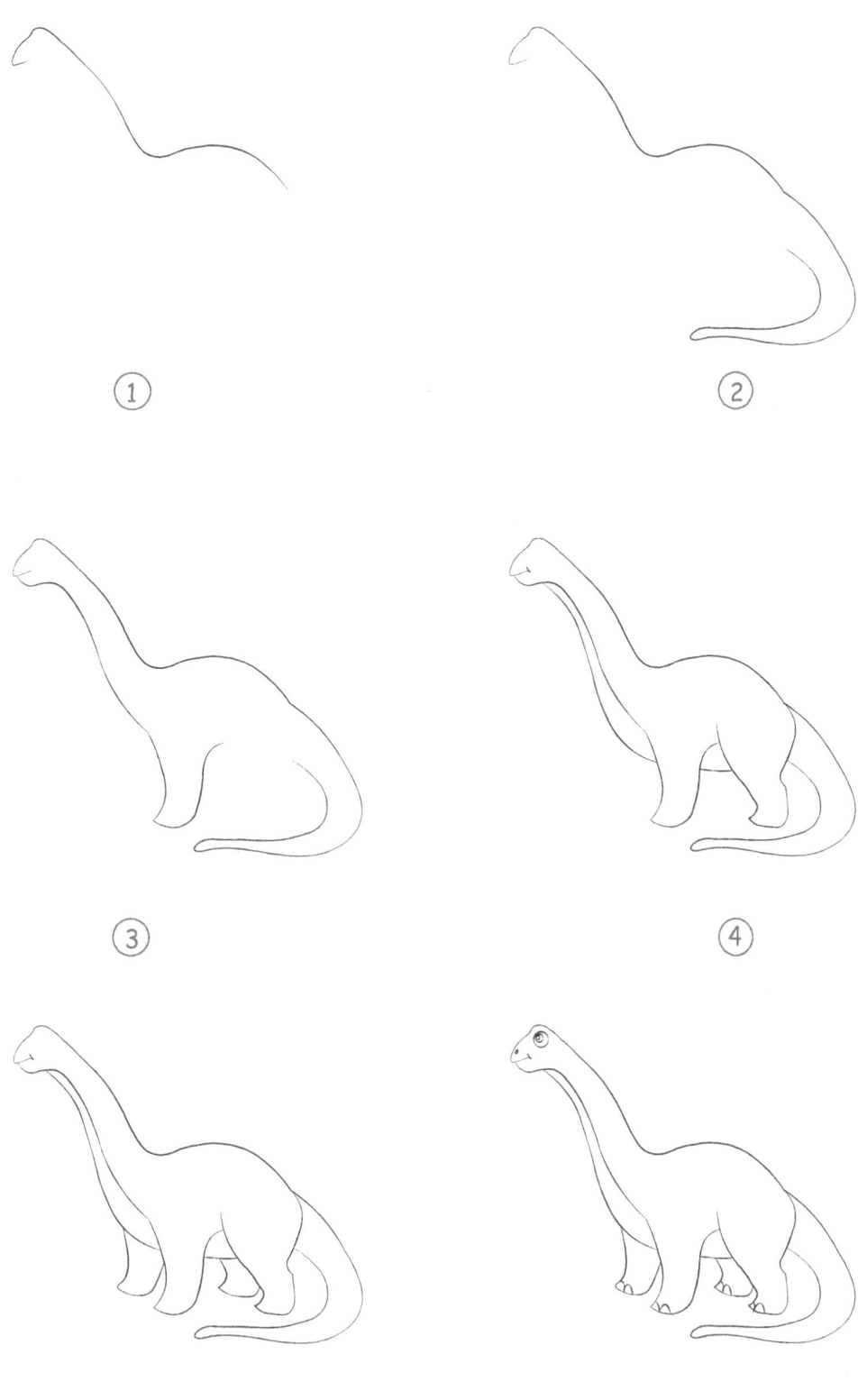

① ② ③ ④ ⑤ ⑥

STEP BY STEP
HIPO

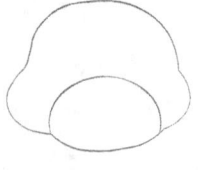

①

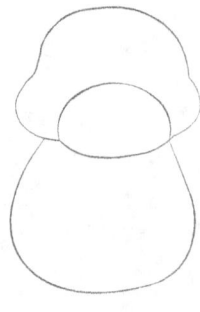

②

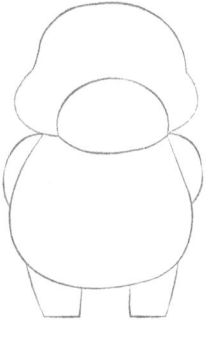

③

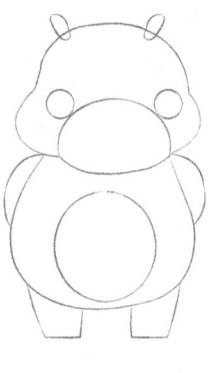

④

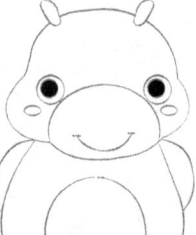

⑤

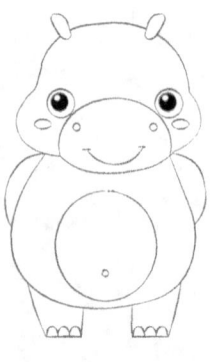

⑥

STEP BY STEP
FISH

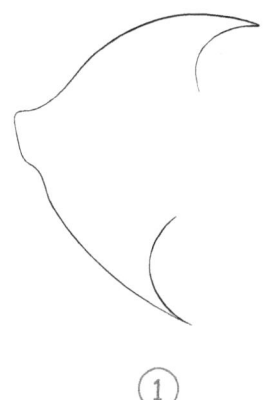

①

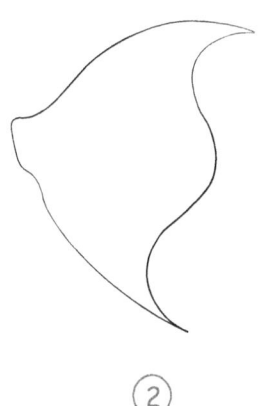

②

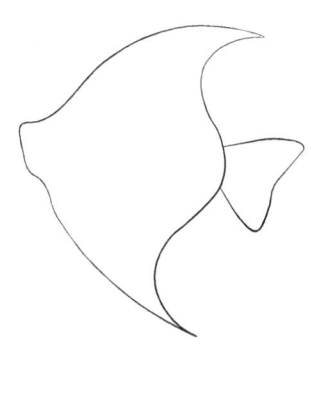

③

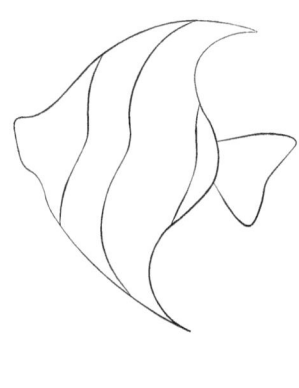

④

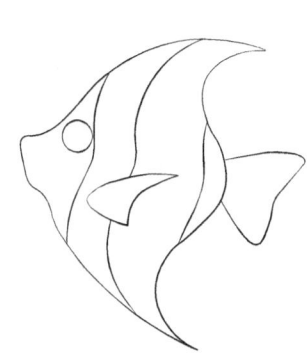

⑤

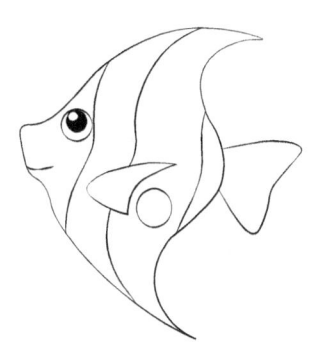

⑥

STEP BY STEP
SEAL

① ②

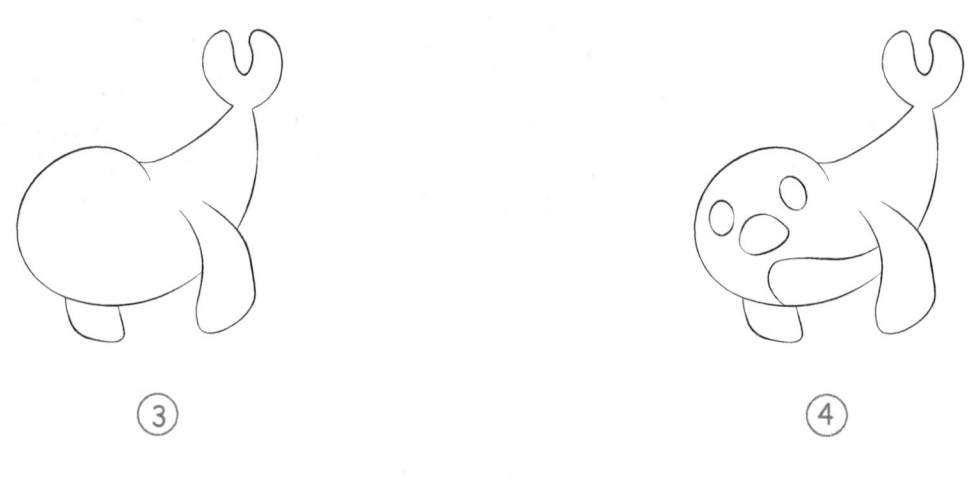

③ ④

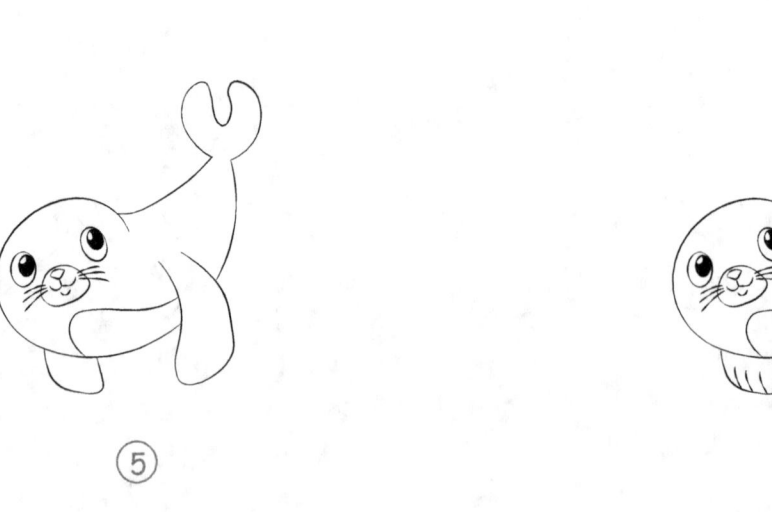

⑤ ⑥

STEP BY STEP
SEAHORSE

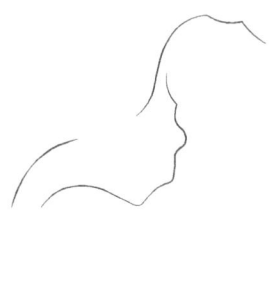

①

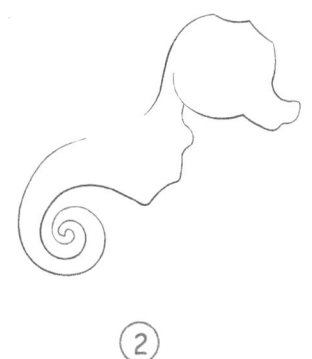

②

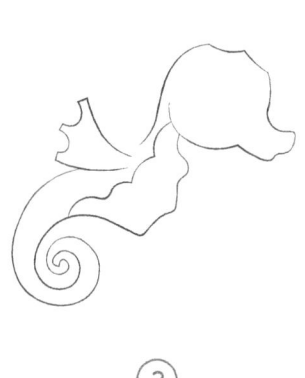

③

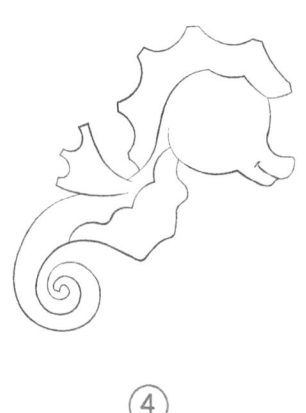

④

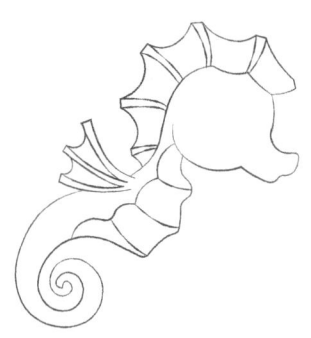

⑤

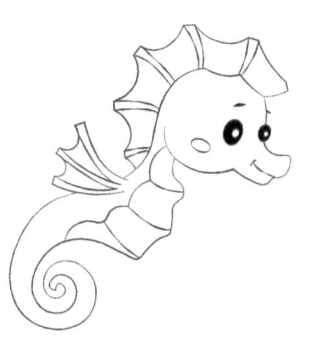

⑥

STEP BY STEP
SNAKE

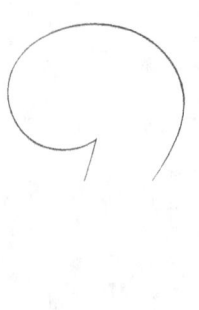

①

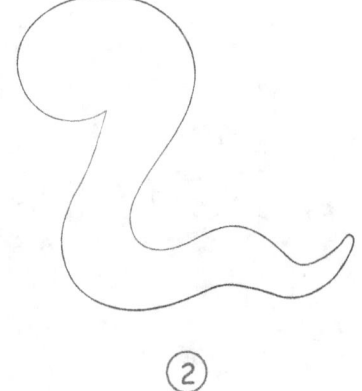

②

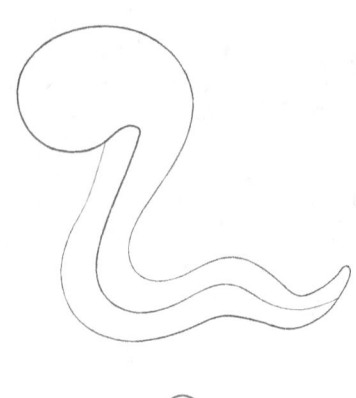

③

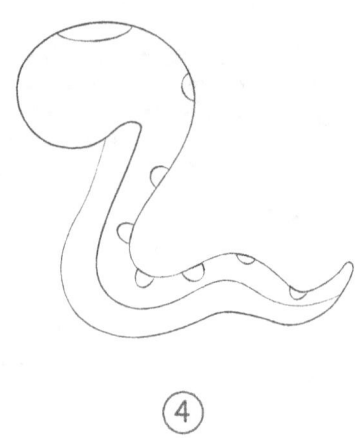

④

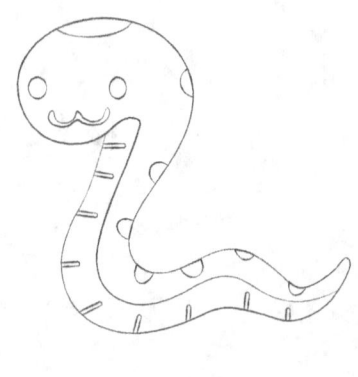

⑤

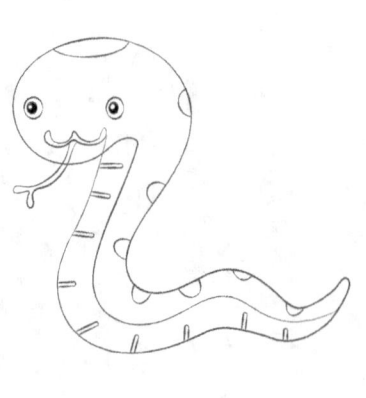

⑥

www.ingramcontent.com/pod-product-compliance
Lightning Source LLC
Chambersburg PA
CBHW082220290526
45794CB00009B/3607